PUFFIN BOOKS

HOW WE KNOW WHAT WE KNOW

Shruthi Rao (http://shruthi-rao.com) has a master's degree in energy engineering and worked in the IT industry before she started writing. She is the author of *10 Indian Women Who Were the First to Do What They Did* (2019, Duckbill), *20 Indians Who Changed the World* (2019, Talking Cub), *Susie Will Not Speak* (2018, Duckbill), *Manya Learns to Roar* (2017, Duckbill), *The Secret Garden* (2016, NSI), *Avani and the Pea Plant* (2016, Pratham), among others. She lives in the San Francisco Bay Area, and loves books, desserts, trees, benches, science and long walks.

HOW WE KNOW WHAT WE KNOW

Fascinating Stories of Discovery and Invention

SHRUTHI RAO

Illustrations by Sumedha Sah

PUFFIN BOOKS

An imprint of Penguin Random House

To my parents
Brinda and Nagraj Rao
for teaching me to dig deeper

PUFFIN BOOKS

USA | Canada | UK | Ireland | Australia
New Zealand | India | South Africa | China

Puffin Books is part of the Penguin Random House group of companies
whose addresses can be found at global.penguinrandomhouse.com

Published by Penguin Random House India Pvt. Ltd
7th Floor, Infinity Tower C, DLF Cyber City,
Gurgaon 122 002, Haryana, India

Published in India in Puffin Books by Penguin Random House India 2021

Text copyright © Shruthi Rao 2021
Illustration copyright © Sumedha Sah 2021

All rights reserved

10 9 8 7 6 5 4 3 2 1

The views and opinions expressed in this book are the author's own and the
facts are as reported by her which have been verified to the extent possible,
and the publishers are not in any way liable for the same.

ISBN 9780143449737

Book design by Antra K
Typeset in Baskerville by Manipal Technologies Limited, Manipal
Printed at Replika Press Pvt. Ltd, India

www.penguin.co.in

CONTENTS

INVENTIONS

IDEAS THAT CHANGED THE WORLD

MODERN LIFE AND LATEST DISCOVERIES

SOMETHING OF TOTAL ACCEPTANCE

INTRODUCTION

The sun shines down on your shoulders as you walk home. Phew, it's hot. You reach home, throw your bag down and have a quick wash. You open the refrigerator and pour yourself a glass of cool lemonade. You turn on the fan and plonk down on your chair. You take a few gulps of lemonade and place the glass on the table. The droplets on the glass light up as the sun's rays pass through them. What a beautiful sight! You take out your phone, snap a picture of the glass of lemonade and send it to a friend, before you glug the lemonade down.

A regular, humdrum scene? Now, let us just go back to the beginning and look at all the things we have taken for granted and see what we know about them.

Do we know what the sun is? What is it made up of? Why do we feel hot? What exactly is temperature? When and why did we start measuring it? When you dropped the bag, why did it fall down, and not go upwards instead? What on earth is gravity? Who invented the refrigerator? Are the lemons in the lemonade good for us? How does flicking a switch turn on the fan? What is electricity? Who discovered it? What is air? How can you feel something you cannot see? Why did those droplets form on the outside of the glass of lemonade? Who made the first smartphone? Who took the first photograph? How am I able to upload a picture online or send it to a friend? What is the Internet? Who discovered it? Why? How? What? Where? When?

Okay, maybe not those many questions. But the good news is that when you do have such questions, you'll find the answers to many of them at your fingertips—in books or on the Internet.

But how do we know all this? Who were the men and women who found answers to these questions? What made them go looking for these answers in the first place?

The human brain loves a good puzzle. The spotting of a problem, the scratching of heads, the hunt for the solution, and finally, the wonderful moment when the truth or solution is revealed to us. That is why puzzles are so popular, and also why good mystery books are unputdownable.

This very sense of mystery and wonder is what propelled scientists to go after solutions to puzzling questions and annoying problems. Sometimes, they discovered the answers by accident. At other times, they kept working at a problem for decades until they reached the solution.

Some of these scientists received praise, fame and awards. Others were rebuked and ridiculed. Some lost their reputation, others their wealth. A few were even put to death for going against the word of the authorities of the day. But nothing (except being dead) deterred them from going after the truth.

This book is full of such stories of men and women who worked tirelessly to discover how things work, and invented gadgets that made our lives better. It is thanks to them that we now know what we know.

But why do we need to know these stories?

Well, such stories teach us how to recognize puzzles and look for answers. They show us the right methods of discovering the truth. In other words, these stories demonstrate how science works. They show us that the scientific method is the only one we can rely on to solve many of the world's problems.

And boy, the world has some big problems. Consider climate change for instance. The evidence is clear that the climate is changing (you can read about it in this book). But some people in positions of power, those who have the ability to bring about laws and regulations to prevent further damage to the earth, refuse to acknowledge that climate change is real. These people are essentially rejecting science. Another example is that of anti-vaxxers: Putting their faith in an old paper that was later conclusively proved wrong, these people believe that vaccinations are harmful. By not vaccinating their children, they have brought back diseases such as measles, which had been nearly eradicated. Their rejection of science and evidence ends up affecting other people too.

Science does not always have all the answers. But science knows how to look for answers. Science needs curious, open-minded people, unafraid to ask questions and demand proof, like the people in the pages of this book. And that is why we need stories like these, because they will remind us again of the wonder and the magic of invention and discovery. They tell us what it took to get to where we are, and what we need to do to move forward.

I hope you have as much fun reading and learning as I had researching and writing it!

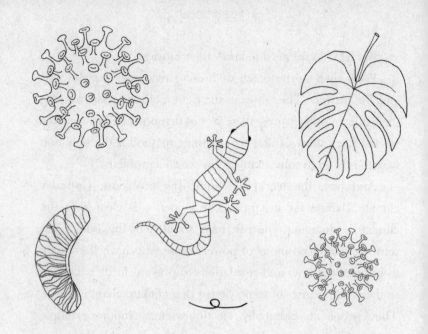

ALL THINGS ALIVE

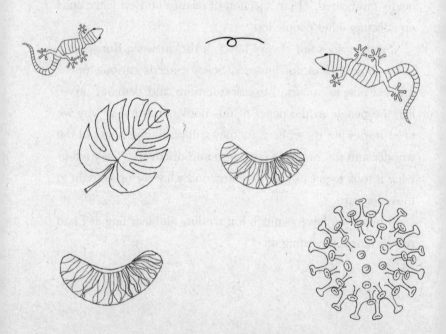

How to Make Mice and Scorpions, and Other Strange Ideas

SPONTANEOUS GENERATION

How do you make a mouse? Stuff a dirty shirt into the mouth of a container of wheat and leave it in a dark corner.

How do you make a scorpion? Sandwich basil leaves between two bricks, leave it out in the sun, and wait.

No, this isn't a fantasy novel. These were actual 'recipes' offered in the seventeenth century by the scientist Jan Baptista van Helmont.

It sounds unbelievable, but there was a time when humans thought that living things arose out of non-living sources: that butterflies just emerged fully formed from mud, oysters appeared from the sea, lice sprang from dirt or sweat, flies came out from meat and wasps from trees! This is known as the theory of spontaneous generation, which states that inanimate objects can bring life forms into being.

1

But in the seventeenth century, Italian naturalist Francesco Redi was having none of it. How could maggots just arise from rotting meat? Redi placed some meat in a covered jar and some in an uncovered jar, and left them alone. In a few days, the uncovered meat, which in the meantime had been visited by flies, was crawling with maggots, while the covered meat wasn't. Could the maggots be related to flies in any way? Or was it due to something present in the air?

In his next experiment, Redi placed some meat in an uncovered jar as before. He put the rest of the meat into a jar, which he covered with a muslin cloth. Muslin kept flies away, but let in air. (We must pause here and appreciate his scientific method—approaching the problem step by step, eliminating each option one by one.) In a few days, once again, the uncovered meat was full of maggots, while the one covered with muslin wasn't.

Redi concluded that flies laid eggs from which maggots were born. But the idea of spontaneous generation was so widespread that scientists rushed to prove him wrong with their half-baked experiments.

Meanwhile, Maria Sibylla Merian, a seventeenth-century naturalist and artist, somehow managed to take time away from raising a large family to study nature. She spent hours observing insects, and made the most elaborate and realistic drawings that showed how insects reproduced, what they ate and what their life cycle was. She was so committed to her work that she sometimes stayed up all night waiting for a butterfly to emerge from its pupa so that she could sketch it. Merian took long voyages to tropical places, such as Suriname, and recorded her observations of the creatures that inhabited those lands. She published her artwork to admiring audiences who were not only dumbstruck by her talent but by this astounding look into the private lives of little creatures, with the laying and hatching of eggs clearly sketched out. She was one of the first people to provide evidence against the theory of spontaneous generation. And yet, the idea held on.

Once microscopes were invented, scientists were able to observe microorganisms. They applied the theory of spontaneous generation to microbes too. Throughout the eighteenth century, scientists conducted experiments to either prove or disprove how microbes are generated, or spread.

The argument raged on until 1864, when Louis Pasteur conducted his landmark experiments. Pasteur took broth—a liquid with nutrients used in experiments to grow bacteria—in two flasks. One flask had a straight vertical neck, with an open mouth. The second flask had an S-shaped neck. The idea of the S-shaped neck is that dust and other particles from outside would get trapped in the bends of the neck, and would not reach the round bottom of the flask. Pasteur boiled both broths to make sure that all microbes in them were killed, and then placed them side by side. After a few days, the broth in the straight-necked flask became cloudy, indicating the growth of microbes. The broth in the flask with the S-shaped neck was still clear. If spontaneous generation was true, microbes should have grown in both broths. With this experiment, the argument was put to rest.

DID YOU KNOW?

Some of the greatest minds accepted the theory of spontaneous generation without questioning. They included Isaac Newton (of gravity fame), William Harvey (who discovered how the body circulates blood) and philosopher René Descartes. Jan Baptista van Helmont himself was a scientist you'll meet in the next article—he conducted a landmark experiment in the quest to know where plants get their food.

What Do Plants Eat?

How do trees grow? What do they eat? Soil, perhaps? Well, that's what the ancient Greeks thought anyway.

About 400 years ago, Jan Baptista van Helmont undertook a five-year experiment. He started with a small willow tree that weighed less than a newborn baby. He took some soil, dried it thoroughly and weighed it. He planted the tree in this soil, carefully watered the soil over the course of five years and did not let any dust or particles fall on the soil. At the end of five years, he gently uprooted the tree and weighed it. The tree, which had started off weighing about as much as a baby, now weighed as much as a large adult.

Then he dried out the soil and weighed it. The soil weighed almost exactly the same as when he started. Conclusion: The tree definitely did not devour the soil.

Van Helmont concluded that the weight of the plant must have come from water.

It was Joseph Priestley who, over 250 years ago, gave us the first clue that there was a connection between plants and gases. Priestley placed a burning candle in a sealed box. The candle soon burnt out. But when he introduced a plant into the sealed box, he was able to light the candle again. Similarly, he put a mouse in a sealed jar, and the mouse lost consciousness after a while. But when he put the mouse in the sealed jar along with a plant, the mouse stayed alert.

Priestley concluded that plants released a gas that was essential for fire to burn, and for animals to live. But what was it, and why did plants release it?

Jan Ingenhousz, a Dutch scientist, conducted a set of experiments in the late 1770s. He submerged various plants into water and observed them in darkness, in sunlight and during the day as well as the night.

Amid his frantic experimentation, one thing stood out: Little bubbles formed on the submerged plants—but only when the plants were in sunlight.

He concluded from his observations that plants make use of sunlight to produce these little bubbles of gas. This gas was what allowed a mouse to survive and a candle to burn. He also noticed that the bubbles were formed in the green areas of the plant, and not so much in the non-green areas, such as the woody parts of the plant.

It took some more scientists to zero in on the actual process. Jean Senebier, a Swiss scientist, found that when plants grow, their carbon content increases. He said this must be because they absorb carbon dioxide. C.B. van Niel, an American biologist, concluded that water and sunlight are both needed to make food, and carbon dioxide is absorbed and oxygen released in the process.

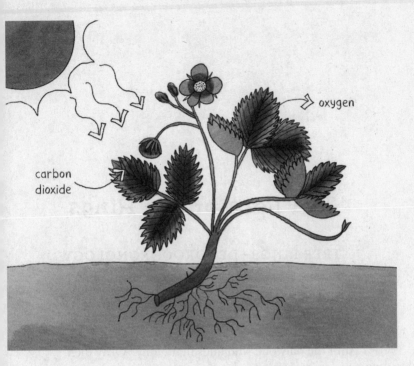

carbon
dioxide

oxygen

Now we know that plants use sunlight to make food from carbon dioxide and water. The process is known as photosynthesis (photo—light, synthesis—creating).

DID YOU KNOW?

Plants are not the only ones that perform photosynthesis! Some single-celled organisms are photosynthetic too, but so are some multicellular organisms. There is a sea slug that consumes algae, which are not digested. They remain in the creature's system and provide food for the slug through photosynthesis. There is also a kind of hornet that uses sunlight to generate electricity.

The Lore of the Rings

How do you find out the age of a tree?

Ask it politely.

Am I the only one who finds that funny? Okay then.

We can figure out the age of a tree by counting its rings. Dendrochronology is a method by which we can find out the exact date when a tree ring was formed.

As a tree grows, not only does its height increase, but also its girth. Each year, it adds another layer, called a cambium layer, to itself. When you cut a tree horizontally, you see alternating light and dark circles. These are tree rings. The light circles mark the growth of the tree in spring, and the dark circle in winter. So, one dark circle and one light circle constitute one year in the tree. (Not always though! Not all species of trees tell their age accurately through rings.)

Tree rings tell us a lot of stories, much more than just the age of a tree. How did we figure out that the rings of a tree hold so many stories? And how did we extract these stories from them?

In the fourth century BCE, the Greek botanist Theophrastus wrote that trees produce new rings each year. About 500 years ago, Leonardo da Vinci wrote that the width of the ring can tell us about the weather conditions of that year. If there is a lot of rainfall, the rings are wider. If there is drought, the trees don't grow much, and the ring is narrow.

In the 1700s, French scientists with the magnificent names of Henri Louis Duhamel du Monceau and Georges-Louis Leclerc, Comte de Buffon studied the effect of weather conditions on tree rings. In many trees, a certain ring stood out clearly. This ring corresponded to the year 1709, and was caused by frost damage, which all the trees experienced. The scientists used this ring as a marker. Whenever they encountered this kind of ring in any tree, they knew immediately that this was the 1709 ring. They could then count other rings with this ring as the base.

By locating unique rings and patterns in tree rings, they could note down precisely which ring was made in which year. So, when they came across a new section of wood, they only had to glance at the rings and they would recognize them like you recognize a face, and tell you when the rings were created!

In the 1800s, a brilliant idea occurred to Alexander Catlin Twining, an American. Because humans started recording data about weather and climate only recently, we have no idea how the climate in the world was in the past. So, wondered Twining, what if we study the rings of very old trees to figure out how the climate was in ancient times? Sounds exciting? It is! Even today, scientists use dendrochronology to study climate change.

A similar idea occurred to Andrew Ellicott Douglass, an American astronomer. Environmental conditions affect what a ring looks like. The sun goes through a lot of variation in its intensity. Do these solar cycles affect tree rings? Can you tell in which years the sun shone particularly brightly, just by looking at tree rings?

He made a detailed study of trees. He was meticulous, patient and had a great memory; so he was perfectly suited for the job. He never did find the answer to his original question, but instead, he laid the foundation of dendrochronology as a science. He had a massive collection of sets of tree rings. He got access to a giant sequoia in California, which was 3000 years old, and was able to study and record tree rings going back to 1305 BCE!

Dendrochronology is used in a number of fields; for instance, archaeologists use it to date historic sites. The rings in the wood used in a historic building will tell you when the tree was cut down, which will give you an idea of when that building was built!

DID YOU KNOW?

You need not cut down a tree in order to count its rings. You can use an instrument called a borer to bore into the tree, and bring out a little tube of the tree. This tube of wood has all the rings in it. And it causes minimal damage to the tree.

Scientists have created tree-ring sequences as long as 12,460 years! Now, they don't just measure the width of the rings. They also have ways to measure the density of the wood, the chemicals in each ring, and so on. The stories only get better and more detailed as technology advances.

Eat Them Lemons, Ye Scurvy Dog!

Sailors of the seventeenth and eighteenth centuries were a gnarly, tough lot. Not only did they have the gumption to sail to unexplored destinations on stormy seas for months on end (with no Global Positioning System, i.e., GPS)—but they had to survive terrible diseases that had no cure—like scurvy.

Whether as an insult or a disease, scurvy ruled the lives of these sailors. Their gums bled and their teeth fell out (with no tooth-fairy benefits). Their wounds and sores didn't heal and their muscles weakened until they died. Scurvy killed more sailors than wars or shipwrecks did. Sometimes, on really long voyages, two out of three sailors died of scurvy by the time they reached their destination.

And the worst part? Nobody knew what caused scurvy, or how to cure it.

Many tried weird cures, but failed. Those captains would have paid you in gold if you could tell them how to cure scurvy.

In 1747, James Lind, a Scottish surgeon, hopped on board the HMS *Salisbury*. He conducted a series of experiments on the sailors. He selected sailors stricken with scurvy and divided them into six groups. He fed the first group their usual diet. He gave four of the remaining groups different supplements such as cider, vinegar, seawater and so on. The sixth group got oranges and lemons in addition to their regular diet. All the supplements were random choices, except perhaps oranges and lemons; there had been unconfirmed reports that these fruits helped cure scurvy.

Surprise! The soldiers who ate oranges and lemons made a dramatic recovery from scurvy—in just six days. The other groups showed no improvement.

Unfortunately, James Lind did not publicize his findings. Besides, he made another mistake. Since it was difficult to keep fruits fresh, he heated orange juice to make a concentrate, in order to preserve it. On future voyages, he took these concentrates aboard ships as a treatment for scurvy. But heating destroys vitamins and he didn't know that! The 'treatment' did not work.

Three decades later, Gilbert Blane, a British physician, conducted more studies like Lind's and confirmed Lind's discovery. He introduced lemons and limes into the diet of British sailors, and there was a remarkable improvement in their health. In fact, 'limey' became a slang term for British sailors.

It was only in the 1900s that scientists discovered what vitamins are, and how essential they are for our body. Now we know that it is a lack of Vitamin C in the body that causes scurvy. The human body uses Vitamin C to make collagen, a protein that acts as a glue that binds together the body's muscles and blood vessels. Without Vitamin C, tissues decay and disintegrate, and these cause the symptoms of scurvy.

Easily kept at bay by listening to your adults for once and chomping down on fresh fruit regularly.

So now we know why sailors suffered from scurvy! Fruit wasn't a part of their diet at sea. After all, fruits rot quickly and there were no refrigerators back then. Sailors mostly ate biscuits, dried and salted fish and meat—not a great source of vitamins.

DID YOU KNOW?

James Lind's experiment was the first instance
of a controlled trial in history. In controlled
trials, people are allocated to groups randomly
and given different treatments, so as to compare
and contrast the result of the treatment. Most
importantly, there is also a control group, in this
case, the sailors who were not given any extra
supplements. These kinds of trials form the basis
for nearly every kind of research today. Though
it seems pretty obvious to us nowadays, such
disciplined trials and experiments had neither
been conducted nor documented before.

Awake or Asleep?

We spend one-third of our lives sleeping. If you are twelve years old, you have slept away four years of your life! But you can't call it wasted time. The body and the brain rest and rejuvenate during sleep. Sleep is a very important part of our lives, but until about seventy years ago, we knew next to nothing about sleep. Most scientists thought that the brain shuts off, and we sleep, that's all!

Sleep by itself wasn't a subject of interest, but many were curious about the daily cycles of life. For example, Jean Jacques d'Ortuous de Marian, an astronomer, studied plants in the eighteenth century. Some plants open their leaves when there is sunlight, and close them at night when it is dark. He put the plants in a completely dark place—and saw that they opened and closed their leaves at the right times even in complete darkness. This meant they had some kind of an internal clock that was not dependent on sunshine. Other scientists discovered that animals had such cycles too.

What is the best way to study sleep in humans? Put yourself through torturous situations. Well, that's what Nathaniel

Kleitman did in the twentieth century. He was the first scientist to study sleep in a methodical way. He had volunteers, but he used himself as a lab rat quite often. To observe how it would affect him, Kleitman once stayed awake for 115 hours—that's nearly five days and nights without sleep!

Kleitman wanted to find out if the twenty-four-hour cycle was natural. Was this cycle in response to day and night? Is this a habit, and can we change it? He observed the sleep habits of residents of the Arctic regions, where it is dark for six months in a year, and people who live for long periods in submarines, where there is no real concept of night and day.

Kleitman put himself to the test again. He and his student decided to live in complete darkness in Mammoth Cave, Kentucky. They set up beds in a large chamber 140 feet underground. To reach this chamber, they had to cross rocky underground jungles and a subterranean river. They stayed in this cold, dark cave for 32 days. They slept for 9 hours each 'day', worked for 10 hours, rested for 9 more hours. They wanted to see if they could keep up this 28-hour cycle, instead of a 24-hour one. His student, who was in his twenties, adapted to the cycle within a week. But Kleitman, at forty-three, couldn't.

Kleitman continued to study sleep in the world's first sleep laboratory, which he established at the University of Chicago. He noted how we sometimes seem to sleep lightly and are woken up by just a small cough next door. At other times, a wedding orchestra could play music at eardrum-bursting decibels right next to you, and you would still not wake up.

He observed that our eyes move sometimes during sleep, and we breathe differently at different stages of sleep. He wanted to know whether we can find out anything about sleep cycles with this information. He assigned this job to his student Eugene

Aserinsky—observe and monitor the eye and body movements of sleeping children.

About thirty years previously, Austrian psychiatrist Hans Berger had discovered EEG or electroencephalogram—a way of recording the electrical activity in the brain by placing electrodes on the scalp. Initially, scientists had laughed at Berger, but they quickly realized that this was a very real measure of what is going on in our heads. An EEG can show what state a person is in—asleep or awake—because the patterns of the EEG are different in each of these stages of the brain.

So, one night, Aserinsky taped electrodes on his eight-year-old son's head, turned on the EEG machine and went to the next room. He observed the patterns the machine printed out on a long sheet of paper. The pattern changed when the boy fell asleep. Suddenly, it changed again, which seemed to indicate that the child was awake. Aserinsky went over to the next room, expecting to see the boy wide awake, but he was fast asleep! Strange. Did the machine malfunction?

Aserinsky spent another night in the same way and once again, he saw patterns associated with wakefulness—only, the boy was asleep. Aserinsky tried this with other people and got the same results. This sleep stage coincided with the time when the sleeping person's eyes made jerky movements under the eyelids, but the person didn't respond when called.

He called this the REM sleep—rapid eye movement. This was a major discovery. Before REM, people thought the brain just switched off like a lamp during sleep. But now they saw that the brain actually had two stages—one was a deep, quiet sleep, known as non-REM sleep, and the other was an active sleep, which was REM sleep. During REM, the brain even consumes oxygen and sugar equal to what a wakeful brain needs!

REM sleep occurs about ninety minutes after you fall asleep. Your eyes move rapidly under closed eyelids. Your breathing is faster too, your heart rate as fast as it would be when you are awake. Dreaming mostly occurs during REM. Your muscles cannot move at this time, to prevent you from enacting your dreams! People remember dreams

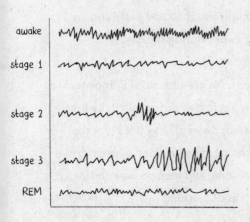

most of the time when they are woken up from REM sleep. Older people spend less time in this active sleep stage.

This discovery helped diagnose and treat sleep disorders that lots of people suffer from. It also told us a lot more about the brain. We still have a lot to learn, though.

DID YOU KNOW?

Have you ever experienced waking up with a jerk just as you are falling asleep? These are called hypnic jerks, or sleep starts. Scientists are not sure why it happens, but there is an interesting theory relating to evolution. When we were primates and nodding off on trees, our brains jerked us awake to warn us that we might fall off the tree!

Our ancestors had different sleeping habits. They used to have periods of rest followed by periods of activity through the day. They moved to a pattern of sleeping at night about 50,000 years ago, by being awake during the day.

There is evidence from pre-industrial Europe that people slept at night in two shifts, called the first sleep and the second sleep. They used to wake up after a few hours, do some kind of activity like reading or sewing, and then go back to sleep until morning.

Wrong on Race

What is your race if you are from India? What about people from Africa? And America? And how about Chinese and Japanese people? And how about . . .

Don't bother with any more questions. We are all the same race. The human race, if you want.

Scientists have found that humans all around the world are genetically very similar—99.9 per cent similar. This means that if you consider a 1000 characteristics, we are similar in 999 ways. So we are more alike than we are different. Yes, in spite of having different skin colours, hair, height and eyes.

Also, race is not biological at all. Race is what is called a social construct—an idea created and accepted by society.

But why did these ideas come about in the first place?

When people used the word 'race' early on, they just meant it to refer to a family or a tribe—basically, a group of people. They did notice that people had different skin colours and concluded that it had some relation with people living in hot or cold places, and that was it. They even thought that skin colour was not permanent—that if a person with dark skin moved to a cold place, their skin would get lighter.

The idea of race began around the eighteenth century, when Carolus Linnacus, a Swedish naturalist, classified the animals and plants of the world into families, groups, species, and so on. He even classified human beings into four varieties—European, American, Asiatic and African.

Scientists had already noted that human beings have the biggest brains in the animal kingdom, and also the most skills. American anthropologist Samuel George Morton used this concept to classify human beings themselves. He measured skulls of people and concluded, with absolutely no evidence, that people with bigger skulls are more superior and more civilized. He classified white people as the best among them all.

Influential people from all fields, like US president Thomas Jefferson, also began saying that some groups of people were superior to others. Since most of these prominent people were white, they put themselves at the highest rung on the ladder and declared themselves gifted with the attributes of beauty, skill and intelligence. They associated other groups with unfavourable characteristics.

This concept was convenient for them. In America, slavery was rampant. Slave masters told themselves that it was just fine to have black slaves and treat them inhumanely; after all, they were inferior, and needed superior beings to look after them. Similarly, when Europeans went around colonizing the world, it was convenient to think that the lands they colonized were full of inferior and uncivilized people. Their attitude was that they were doing the people a favour by colonizing them.

Some scientists protested. German professor Friedrich Tiedemann did not find the tiniest shred of evidence of some people being superior to others.

American sociologist W.E.B. Du Bois wrote that what we call race was just social and cultural differences between people, and that it wasn't biological.

Not many people listened, but after World War II and the mass genocide of Jewish people by Nazis (based on the prevalent concept of race), the world sat up and took notice. The discussion about race became urgent and important.

M.F. Ashley Montagu wrote a book in which he completely demolished the concept of race. Scientists found no evidence of differences in intelligence or ability between people of different 'races'.

As scientists studied genes, they came to know that people across the world have very similar genes. A deeper study of history has also revealed that the ancestors of all the people in the world originated in the same place. They moved to different parts of the world, creating branches of the human race, and then, there was further mixing of these different branches. With this, it becomes clear that any talk about the 'purity' of genes does not make much sense.

An important study on human diversity by Stanford University in 2002 also concluded that we are all more or less the same. There is no indicator in our genes that specifies a person's race.

Today, scientists and sociologists generally agree that race is a social construct, and not derived from biology. Scientists prefer to use the term 'ancestry' instead of race, to talk about diversity.

Despite being 99.9 per cent similar to one another, throughout history, people have used this 0.1 per cent variation as an excuse to discriminate, and to commit all kinds of atrocious acts. What a pity that is!

DID YOU KNOW?

The concept of race is dangerous not just socially, but medically. Many people still believe that some diseases are more common among certain races. For example, doctors have long thought that cystic fibrosis affects white people. If a black person goes to the doctor with symptoms of the disease, some doctors might not even test the person for cystic fibrosis until it is too late.

Terrible Lizards

DINOSAURS

Dinosaurs! Hard to think of a set of creatures that have captured our imaginations the way they have. The best part? We know a whole lot about them without ever having set eyes on real, living dinosaurs. This, of course, is thanks to fossils, which are preserved remains (bones, shells, imprints) of creatures that once lived.

But how did we come to know about dinosaurs in the first place?

Over the centuries, people must have stumbled across dinosaur bones in various geographic locations. They did not know what they were, though. Ancient Chinese records speak of dragon bones, which are most probably dinosaur bones.

The first person to describe and record a dinosaur bone was Robert Plot, the curator of Ashmolean Museum in Oxford. In 1676, Plot found a fossil that looked to him like a thigh bone. An enormous thigh bone. In his book, he concluded that the bone must be from a gigantic ancient human being. He was wrong, of course. Unfortunately, the specimen is now lost. But

Plot recorded where he found it and what it looked like. Since scientists later found dinosaur bones in that same place, we now know what Plot found was indeed a dinosaur bone.

Eventually, fossil hunting became a popular pastime. Rich and fashionable people wanted fossils of ancient plants and other creatures, to add to their private collections. Mary Anning, an English palaeontologist, started off as a fossil hunter in the early nineteenth century to earn a living. But with her keen eye, skill and dedication, she made some very important discoveries of fossils of ichthyosaurs and plesiosaurs, and even a pterodactyl.

Another woman with a similar-sounding name, Mary Ann Mantell, found the tooth of a creature when on a walk in Surrey, England, in 1822. Her husband Gideon Mantell, a geologist, described the tooth in his publications, and later named it *Iguanodon*. The couple discovered even more *Iguanodon* bones, and also those of a *Hylaeosaurus*. Meanwhile, Englishman William Buckland, a professor of geology, found the bones of an animal that seemed to him like an extinct, carnivorous lizard. He named it *Megalosaurus*.

News of these weird fossil finds spread around the world. People were agog with curiosity. But nobody could make head or tail of them—until somebody put the pieces of the puzzle together.

British anatomist Richard Owen came across a chunk of bone in somebody's private collection. It was from the spine of an *Iguanodon*.

He concluded through his observations that the *Megalosaurus*, *Iguanodon* and *Hylaeosaurus* must all be related to each other. The three creatures were very similar to each other, but at the same time, they were different from any other creature that walked the earth. Owen deduced that this group of creatures must have once roamed the earth, but have since disappeared. He called them dinosaurs—terrible lizards.

Imagine the waves of excitement that rippled through the world at the thought of gigantic, strange creatures ambling around like we do now! Naturally, more people wanted in on the action.

Two Americans, O.C. Marsh and E.D. Cope, took it a bit too far. They got into a bitter rivalry now known as the Bone Wars, trying to outdo each other at finding the best dinosaurs. This ugly fight led to their financial ruin, and their penchant for publicly slandering one another damaged their reputations. But in the process, they ended up finding thousands and thousands of fossils. Between them, they discovered 136 new species of dinosaurs!

This turned out to be a good thing not only in the study of dinosaurs, but also in the study of evolution. Charles Darwin, the scientist who proposed the theory of evolution, said that the collections of these two men helped hugely in providing evidence that creatures evolved from other creatures!

Dinosaur study picked up after the 1960s, with the help of new technology and scientific methods. We now know more about these strange and wonderful creatures than ever before. We have also learned that dinosaurs still walk the earth—yes, birds are actually descendants of dinosaurs. Scientists have also recently concluded that dinosaurs themselves had some kind of feathers!

DID YOU KNOW?

Coprolytes/coprolites (meaning dung stone) are pieces of poop that have been fossilized (they turn into minerals, and essentially become rocks). They look like rocks too (and do not stink). Scientists get a lot of information from coprolytes, especially about what the creatures ate. Mary Anning was probably the first person to study coprolytes. She is one of the many women in the world who have most influenced the history of science.

Birds Fly to the
Moon—or Do They?

MIGRATION

We humans and our wonderful imaginations. If we don't know the answer to a question, we make up the most incredible stories to explain it. Until someone comes along who cannot accept those stories and decides to investigate.

Take migration. Birds migrate to different places to find food, better living conditions or to breed. *Of course*, you say? But back then, how could people explain why they saw a bird only in summer and not in winter?

Aristotle thought that swallows and kites hibernate in holes in the ground. He was convinced that redstarts turn into robins in the winter. You can't blame him—redstarts migrated to Africa from Greece, where Aristotle lived, and at the same time, robins migrated to Greece. The two species were never present in the same place at the same time, so this was a convenient explanation.

Not so convenient were the barnacle geese turning up in England out of nowhere. Nobody had seen their eggs. Nobody had seen baby barnacle geese. So, about a 1000 years ago, people believed that these geese grew out of trees. In fact, religious Catholics didn't eat meat on Fridays, but they didn't mind eating barnacle geese, because they didn't consider it flesh—after all, they grew on trees!

Migration was not known even until the sixteenth century, when scientist Charles Morton put forth a theory that birds don't hibernate or turn into other birds; they go away somewhere else.

'Now, whither should these creatures go, unless it were to the moon?' he asked.

That's right. He thought they flew to the moon. He explained that they faced no air resistance, were unaffected by gravity, and that they survived on their excess fat (he was right about the last part!).

In 1890, Danish biologist Hans Christian Cornelius Mortensen fastened a ring with an identifying number and his address on to a bird's leg, and let it fly away. His research associates, or in many cases, the public, would catch the bird, check the tag on the ring, and contact him to tell him which bird it was and where they saw it. This way, he got to know where the birds flew, how long they lived and much more. Mortensen banded or ringed 1550 birds and studied them.

More scientists followed suit. The ringed or banded birds were recaptured in other places, and the results were reported to the banding centre. It was clear from the data that birds migrate regularly. Scientists identified migration routes, and came to know that birds fly astonishing distances. In 1931, the first atlas of bird migration was published.

Banding is a difficult process. Not many banded birds are found. It is not easy to capture birds without hurting them either. But with better, gentler nets, the process is getting easier. When the data does come in, it brings with it a wealth of information! It is possible to find the routes and timing of migrations, get estimates of how long birds live, their rest areas, the places and causes of death, how fast they move, how new birds migrate differently compared to veteran birds—all thanks to local and international banding programmes.

It also provides information that helps in planning for the conservation of birds, and making sure that the sites they use for resting or breeding are safeguarded and preserved.

Satellite tracking has also helped in bird tracking. Tiny transmitters in little bags are strapped to the bodies of the birds. The transmitters send signal to satellites. Each transmitter bag is customized for that particular bird species. The signals from the transmitters help researchers track individual birds. In this method, there is no danger of losing the birds, or the bother of having to capture them. Thermometers and cameras are also added sometimes, along with the transmitters. This has given us a lot of detail on bird behaviour, and revealed previously unknown sites of migration and breeding.

Satellite tracking is expensive, though. Besides, you can't put a transmitter and camera on a teensy-weensy bird and expect it to take off. That is why banding is still popular.

At least we now know that birds don't turn into other birds, or go flying off into space!

DID YOU KNOW?

The Arctic tern is a champion flier; it migrates from pole to pole—from its breeding grounds in the Arctic to the Antarctic regions.

Migratory birds use the stars, sun and the magnetic field of the Earth to navigate.

What Lies Beneath

DEEP SEA EXPLORATION

Here is an amazing fact: We know more about the surface of the moon than we know about the Earth's ocean floor. That's because, with the technology we have now, it is easier to send a person to space than to send them to the bottom of the ocean.

If you go deep underwater, the pressure is like fifty jumbo jets pressing down on you. Besides, it is very dark and very cold. You can't see more than a few feet in front of you even with the best lights.

Even until the middle of the nineteenth century, the deep ocean was a complete mystery to us. It is only in the last 150 years or so that we have come to know a little bit about it—that it is like an otherworldly landscape with mountain ranges and trenches, and a nightmare-inducing variety of weird, creepy, never-before-seen animals, some of which glow in the dark and generate their own light.

For a long time, scientists thought life could not exist deep in the ocean. Sunlight does not penetrate very deep into the ocean. So no sunlight = no plants, and no plants = no animals. Duh!

Initially, scientists connected nets and probes to long lines, dropped them into the ocean and pulled them up to see what the nets had caught. They also used dredges—netted bags—that they dragged across the bottom of the ocean, hoping they would sweep up exciting things.

In 1818, the scientists got a little surprise. British explorer Sir John Ross poked around at a depth of about 2 km under the sea near Greenland, and came up with worms and jellyfish. It was the first time anybody had found evidence of life so deep underwater.

On the other hand, British scientist Edward Forbes went dredging in the Aegean Sea and saw almost no creatures in the deep. Forbes proposed the Azoic (lifeless) theory, also known as the Abyssus (depth) theory. It says that the deeper you go, the lesser life there is.

As it happens, the Aegean Sea has relatively less life, and Forbes's equipment wasn't that good. So it was no surprise that he didn't find anything. But his idea took root, even though John Ross had provided worms and jellyfish as evidence that the theory could not be true.

A few decades later, better dredging equipment became available. Michael Sars, a Norwegian marine biologist, found crinoids (sea lilies, creatures related to starfish) in the seas off the coast of Norway. This was tremendously exciting, because until that time, only the fossils of crinoids had been found, and scientists thought they were extinct!

Sars's discoveries helped kick off international deep-sea dredging expeditions. The most important among these was the famous Challenger Deep expedition. Undertaken between 1872 and 1876, it was the first one organized specifically to obtain data about the ocean—temperatures, chemistry of seawater, ocean currents, underwater life and the features of the ocean floor. The ship had labs and the latest scientific equipment. The scientists on board found many species of life uniquely adapted to live on the bottom of the ocean floor.

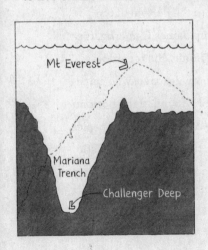

One of the biggest discoveries it made was the Mariana Trench in the Pacific Ocean, the deepest part of the earth. The researchers weren't expecting that much depth. The first time they tried to measure it, they ran out of measuring rope. Then they tried to send a thermometer down. It cracked!

The lowest point of the Mariana Trench is now called the Challenger Deep and is nearly 11 km deep. It is deeper than Mt Everest is high!

In 1977, scientists made another thrilling discovery on the Pacific Ocean floor near the Galapagos Islands. They found hydrothermal vents—slits in the floor from which hot seawater and minerals are released. They look like little volcanoes.

The space around these vents are teeming with life, like fish, clams, mussels, shrimp and crab, even though there's no sunlight. Bacteria-like organisms called archaea turn chemicals, like sulphur released from the vents, into energy. Other creatures live on these archaea.

Scientists think it is possible that life on earth began at hydrothermal vents. There is much to study yet about these vents—scientists are studying the organisms that live here, because it is possible that they hold answers to some of our health and medicine needs!

DID YOU KNOW?

The first solo dive to the bottom of the Challenger Deep was by James Cameron, the director of the film *Titanic*. His record was broken recently by Victor Vescovo, who came back with news of what he found in the bottom-most part of the ocean—an exciting new species of animal? No. Hidden treasure? No. A plastic bag. That's right. We've succeeded in polluting the farthest reaches of our oceans.

Don't Touch That!

The moment a super contagious and dangerous disease makes an appearance around the world, we do everything we can to stay away from the disease. But there are some people who cannot afford to do that—doctors and nurses, and researchers who study the disease to find a cure, as we saw during the COVID-19 pandemic. Imagine the kind of risks they take each day for the cause of science and medicine!

In today's world, these professionals are provided with Personal Protective Equipment (PPE) to protect themselves from infection. They handle samples of infected blood with the utmost care, with multiple levels of protection, away from the public. But what did they do before modern technology? What if they needed to handle samples they had no idea were massively dangerous?

Ebola is a highly contagious disease that affects people in villages mainly in Central and West Africa. It causes fever, aches, weakness and bleeding. Nine out of ten people affected with Ebola die.

Ebola was discovered in 1976. Jean-Jacques Muyembe-Tamfum, a Congolese microbiologist, was studying viral outbreaks at the time. He had heard of an outbreak of a mysterious disease in a Belgian mission in the northern part of the Democratic Republic of Congo (DRC). He travelled to the village along with other scientists, to investigate. When Muyembe-Tamfum tried to draw blood from patients, they bled profusely from the puncture wounds. Gloves were not common then, and Muyembe-Tamfum's hands and fingers got covered with blood, which he washed off well with soap and water.

Muyembe-Tamfum realized that this was not a disease known to humans, and would require more research. He would have to send some samples to the lab for testing. He drew some blood from a sick Belgian nun, and put two vials of this blood into an ordinary shiny blue thermos flask, the kind you use to keep food or drink hot or cold. He filled the flask with ice, closed it and handed it to a passenger flying to Belgium. That person then put the thermos into an ordinary carry-on bag, and travelled on an ordinary commercial aircraft. (Did you cringe with horror?) The samples were then delivered to the Institute of Tropical Medicine at Antwerp, Belgium.

Peter Piot was one of the scientists who received the thermos. The scientists opened the lid, and saw that one of the vials of blood had shattered. The other vial floated in a slush of infected blood and ice. The scientists groped around in the viral mess, wearing only thin latex gloves, trying to pick up the intact vial. A little later, when they received some more samples of blood from the region of the outbreak, one of the scientists dropped a vial on the floor and the contents splattered all over the floor and the researchers' shoes. They cleaned it up as best they could.

They tested the blood samples for known diseases like yellow fever and dengue. No luck. The size of the virus was shockingly large, bigger than anything they'd known. It was a lot like the deadly Marburg virus, which had killed lab workers in Germany nine years previously.

They finally realized the seriousness of the situation. This was no ordinary disease. It was probably now that they realized the risk they'd been taking by not handling the samples carefully.

Further tests were needed. They sent across the samples to what is now known as the CDC (Centers for Disease Control and Prevention) in Atlanta, US. This time, they shipped the samples carefully, in tightly sealed containers. The scientists at CDC confirmed that it was a new, unknown virus.

Over the decades, several more outbreaks have occurred with different Ebola strains. The latest, as of 2019, has affected two provinces in the eastern part of DRC. Unfortunately, violence and conflict are raging in these areas, and it has become difficult to fight or contain the disease. Talk about multiple miseries all at once.

Until very recently, there were no drugs to overcome Ebola, though scientists have been trying to treat it by modified forms of known drugs. But researchers announced in August 2019 that they have had a breakthrough that will hopefully help contain Ebola.

'From now on, we will no longer say that Ebola is not curable.' Guess who said this. The head of the DRC's National Institute for Biomedical Research in Kinshasa—Jean-Jacques Muyembe-Tamfum. Yes, the same person we met at the beginning of this story. Luckily, he washed his hands well back then. If not, he wouldn't have been around to study Ebola for forty-three years, as he has been doing!

DID YOU KNOW?

Ebola is named after the river Ebola, near the Belgian mission where the disease was first noted. Evidence suggests that fruit bats act like a reservoir of the Ebola virus, and it is transmitted to humans from these bats.

THE WORLD AROUND US

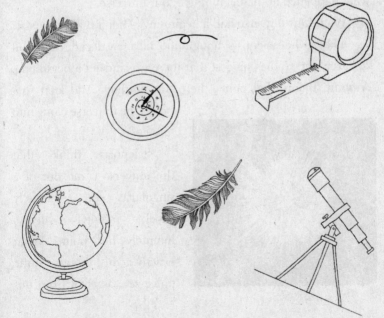

It All Started with a Big Bang

What is the Big Bang? The sound you hear when you burst a big balloon?

Umm, no. The Big Bang Theory is an attempt to explain what happened at the beginning of our universe.

Wait. Our universe had a beginning? Didn't it always exist?

That's what scientists thought too, till a few decades ago. But research and studies suggest that there was indeed a beginning. A point. Before that point, there was nothing. And after that point, the universe came into existence.

Scientists think that the universe came out of a singularity—an infinitely small, infinitely dense, infinitely hot point. What exactly is this, though? If the universe was born from this singularity, where did the singularity come from? Why did it appear?

We don't know that. Yet.

But how do we know that this is what happened?

The story began about a 100 years ago, with Georges Lemaître of Belgium. Though he was an officer of the church, he was fascinated by physics and he studied Albert Einstein's theories of space and time and gravitation. He concluded that if Einstein's theories were right, it meant that the galaxies in the universe are moving away from each other. Lemaître said this proved that the universe is not just static and unmoving, as everybody previously thought. It was expanding.

It was a theory, and though Lemaître had come up with it on the basis of an established theory, scientists needed other proof before they could accept it. But Lemaître didn't have any data to support this idea.

Meanwhile, American astronomer Henrietta Leavitt came up with a way to calculate how far away stars are from Earth. Using her work, astronomer Edwin Hubble looked through his telescope and calculated the distances of various stars from Earth. He concluded that things in the universe were moving away from Earth. Not just that, things that were farther away from Earth were moving away faster than things close to Earth. This could only mean one thing. The universe is indeed expanding. Georges Lemaître was right.

Okay. The universe is expanding. But how does that prove there was a Big Bang?

If the universe is expanding, it must have expanded from some point. Think of the expanding universe as a movie. The galaxies are moving outwards, away from each other. Now run that movie backwards. You can imagine it as the galaxies rushing towards each other. So then, all the galaxies must meet at some point. At this point, all the matter of the universe must have been contained in a very small space, that is, the singularity.

The moment at which this singularity started expanding is the Big Bang.

But where was the proof?

Decades later, in 1965, two scientists, Arno Allan Penzias and Robert Woodrow Wilson, were trying to measure radio signals in the empty space between galaxies. They used a giant horn-shaped antenna, called the Holmdel Horn Antenna, in their observatory at Bell Labs in New Jersey, USA. But as they tried to take measurements, an annoying noise kept interfering, like static on a radio.

Where was this noise coming from?

They pointed the antenna towards New York City. No, it wasn't city noise.

They took measurements of the noise all through the year. No, it didn't change with the seasons.

Could the noise be from a nuclear test that had taken place a while ago? It couldn't be. If it was, the noise should have decreased year by year.

Then what was it?

Perhaps it was just the pigeons roosting in the antenna? They chased away the pigeons, and scooped up and cleaned the droppings. But the noise still remained.

Then they learnt about the scientist Robert Dicke, a professor at Princeton University. Dicke had been thinking about the Big Bang. His opinion was that if the Big Bang was true, there should be some kind of matter remaining from the explosion. And most probably, he said, this would be a kind of low-level background radiation throughout the universe.

Dicke wanted to try and find it. But it turned out that it was exactly what Penzias and Wilson had already found! The hum they had encountered was this very radiation resulting from the Big Bang!

Penzias and Wilson got the Nobel Prize for this discovery, because it proved that the Big Bang Theory was true.

Researchers all over the world are still taking better measurements of this noise, and are finding more things to think about.

DID YOU KNOW?

Because the universe is expanding, eventually, we will not be able to see any other galaxies from Earth or any other spot in the Milky Way. The speed of the outermost galaxies is increasing with time. They will eventually be moving away at the speed of light. So, light from them will never reach us.

Light at the
Bottom of the Well

HOW BIG IS THE EARTH?

Let's say someone asked you to measure the earth. What do you think you would need? Complex instruments, expert advice, maybe satellite images, right? However, 2300 years back, a man measured the circumference of the earth using just his brains, a stick and a hired walker.

Eratosthenes was born in what is now Libya in northern Africa. He was the director of the university at Alexandria in Egypt, when he decided that he wanted to know how big the earth was. The idea that the earth was round, and not flat, had already been around for a while. Pythagoras first proposed it, because he thought that a spherical earth seemed right and beautiful. Aristotle provided proof— ships disappear when they sail over the horizon, the shadow of the earth on the moon during an eclipse is curved, and so on. So, Eratosthenes was convinced of that fact. Now he wanted to find the circumference of the earth. That is the distance you would travel if you started at a point, walked in a straight line around the earth, and reached the same starting point.

There was a well in the Egyptian city of Syene. At noon, on summer solstice (the longest day of the year), the sun's rays lit up the bottom of the well. This meant that the sun was directly above Syene at that time. A pole in the ground didn't create any shadow. But at that same time, the sun was not directly over Alexandria—a pole cast a shadow there.

The key lay in the angle of the shadow of the pole. Angle of the shadow? What's that? When the pole casts a shadow, draw an imaginary line between the tip of the shadow, to the top of the pole. The angle between the pole and this imaginary line is the angle of the shadow.

Eratosthenes measured the angle of the shadow of the pole at Alexandria. It was 7.2 degrees. This is 1/50 of a circle, which has 360 degrees. That meant that the distance between Syene and Alexandria must be 1/50 of the globe. So, if he determined the distance between Syene and Alexandria, he could multiply it by 50 and that would be the size of the earth.

Eratosthenes hired a bematist, a professional walker, trained to walk with equal steps. He sent the bematist to find out the distance between the two cities. The bematist came back with the number. Eratosthenes multiplied that number by 50, and in today's measurements, he got 39,250 km. Guess what the actual circumference of the earth is, as we now know? 40,000 km! Pretty impressive to think that he got this measurement with next to no instruments.

Incidentally, Alexandria wasn't exactly north of Syene, but was on a slightly different longitude. Plus, we now know that the earth is flattened at the poles and bulged at the equator. Eratosthenes didn't know any of this when he made his measurements.

Others had their own ways to measure the earth. In the fifth century CE, Aryabhata calculated the circumference of the earth, most likely by measuring the distance between latitudes. The Arab astronomer Abu Rayhan al-Biruni used trigonometry to calculate the radius of the earth. Both were close to the values that we now know.

In later centuries, especially sixteenth to nineteenth centuries, triangulation was the method used to find distances and areas of lands and countries. (See Mapping Our Way Forward on page 70.)

The Royal Society of London and L'Academie Royale des Sciences in Paris got into a bitter battle with each other at the end of the sixteenth century about the shape of the earth. The French said it was egg-shaped, and the British were convinced it was oblate—flat at the poles, bulged at the equator. Teams were sent out to Peru, near the equator, and to Sweden and Finland at the poles. Measurements proved that the British were right.

Now we have space-based technology and global positioning satellites that help us know the exact dimensions of the earth. It also tells us about minute changes in the earth's surface, right down to the nearest centimetre!

DID YOU KNOW?

Geodesy is a branch of mathematics concerned with the exact size and shape of the earth. It can be very precise. Scientists have long been arguing that the earth is expanding (some say contracting). But recent measurements using geodesy have confirmed that the earth's size remains unchanged.

Slip and Slide

CONTINENTAL DRIFT

Take a look at the world map. See the way the coastlines of South America and Africa match perfectly, as if they are adjacent pieces of a jigsaw puzzle?

More than 100 years ago, a German scientist named Alfred Wegener noticed this too. He wondered if perhaps, long, long ago, all the continents were part of one single landmass. Maybe, he said, they've broken apart and moved away from each other now.

Wegener wasn't the first to notice this, but he was the first to look for more evidence. He observed that many continents separated by large oceans shared similar geographical features. For example, the Appalachian Mountains in North America was similar to the mountains of the Scottish Highlands on the other side of the Atlantic. Rock formations in South Africa matched what he saw in Brazil.

Fossils of tropical plants were present in cold, Arctic regions, where such plants could not possibly have survived. This suggested that these Arctic lands were once located in the tropical regions of the planet!

Armed with all this evidence, Wegener laid forth his theory that the continents have moved, and are still moving. He could not explain why they bothered to move, though.

There was a lot of eye-rolling at Wegener's theory. Was there a way to check if Wegener was right by examining the ocean floor? Perhaps, when the continents moved, they might have left some evidence on the floor. But at that time, there was no way to examine the ocean floor.

During the 1930s, scientists developed an instrument that sent sound waves into the ocean and measured the time it took for the sound to echo back. This told them how deep the ocean was.

They were in for a surprise. It was generally assumed that the ocean floor was smooth. But the echoes showed that the floor was full of trenches, mountains and canyons.

At Columbia University in New York, researcher Bruce Heezen collected the data of the echoes at different places in the ocean. As Marie Tharp, his co-researcher, mapped the data, she noticed something amazing. A massive mountain range, now known as the Mid-Atlantic Ridge, stretched from north to south throughout the Atlantic Ocean. In the midst of this range was a deep valley, where it looked like the floor of the ocean was spreading apart. Bruce Heezen brushed it off as 'girl talk', an insulting term indicating it was unscientific.

At this time, Bell Labs, which did research and development on communication technology, approached them with a problem. The underwater communication cables connecting Europe and America kept snapping somewhere in the Atlantic Ocean and they suspected that it was due to underwater earthquakes. Heezen hired someone to map the earthquakes under the Atlantic Ocean.

Once the earthquake map was ready, Marie Tharp laid it over her ridge map. And it was just like she'd thought—they lined up perfectly! The earthquakes were occurring at the same place as the ridge!

This time, Heezen couldn't ignore her findings. He described them in a talk at Princeton University. In the audience was eminent geologist Harry Hess, who stood up and said excitedly, 'Young man, you have shaken the foundations of geology!'

Harry Hess then published his theory of sea-floor spreading.

Continents sit on plates. The size of the plate does not necessarily coincide with the size of the continent. According to Hess's theory, these plates are moving away from one another. This happens when magma from inside the earth oozes out from between the plates, cools, expands and pushes the plates aside. This way, the space between continents keeps increasing, but

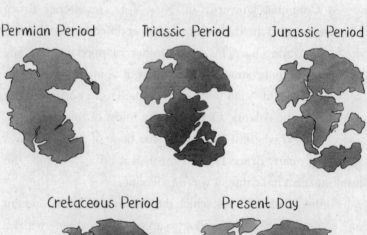

Permian Period   Triassic Period   Jurassic Period

Cretaceous Period   Present Day

the coastlines of the continents will not change in shape. This movement of continents is called Continental Drift.

Scientists also observed that the rocks on either side of the underwater valley were of the same kind. Hot molten magma of Type X must have oozed out from the gap between the plates, settled on either side of the gap, solidified and became rock. Now, magma of Type Y oozed out, pushed aside the Type X rocks (and the plates) and settled on either side of the gap, becoming rocks of Type Y, and so on. So, there are stripes of perfectly matching rocks on either side of the valley! This piece of evidence convinced most geologists, making this theory generally accepted even today.

DID YOU KNOW?

The movement of the plates of the earth is called plate tectonics. The earth's crust is broken into about 8–12 large plates and 20 smaller ones. When two plates clash, they push against each other, causing high mountains to rise. This is how the Himalayas were formed. When two plates brush sideways against each other, earthquakes are caused. The continents are still moving about 1 inch every year, so a map from the future might look very different!

Pangaea was a supercontinent—it broke apart and started moving away to become the world as we now know it.

Here We Go Around the Sun

The moon revolves around Earth, which in turn revolves around the sun along with other planets—any child knows that! But for a long, long time, people believed that the Earth stood stationary at the centre of the universe and all celestial objects revolved around it. Can you blame them? It does seem like the sun, the moon and the stars revolve around Earth every day. Besides, while standing on Earth, you can't feel it moving. It is natural to think that the Earth stands still.

This is what the Greek philosophers Aristotle and Ptolemy believed. The idea is called the geocentric model. (Geo—earth, centric—at the centre.) By the third century BCE, philosophers had concluded that the earth was round, and not flat, as they had previously thought. So they extended that conclusion to other celestial objects too, and concluded, correctly, that the moon, sun and planets were all spheres. They got two things wrong—they still thought the moon, sun and planets revolved around Earth, and they thought these objects moved in circular orbits.

But this doesn't mean that nobody had ever thought of the possibility that Earth was the one that revolved around the sun. Aristarchus of Samos (third century BCE), Greek astronomer Seleucis (second century BCE), Indian astronomer Aryabhata (fifth century CE) and several Arab astronomers also proposed the heliocentric (Helios—sun) model.

But the West was where science flourished in later centuries, and Western scientists tended to follow the work of Greek philosophers. So, until about 500 years ago, most people were convinced that Earth was at the centre of the universe.

With the geocentric model, there was a strange thing astronomers could not explain. Once every two years, Mars, moving in one direction, seemed to slow down and stop. Then it started sauntering in the opposite direction. Astronomers call this retrograde motion. Why did Mars behave so weirdly, like it was lost, or had one drink too many? Astronomers were left scratching their heads.

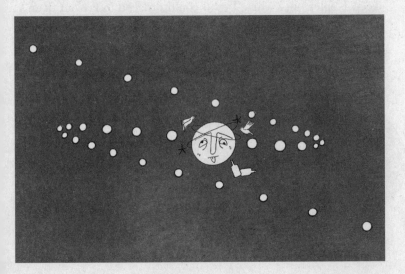

Finally, Polish astronomer Nicolaus Copernicus, in the sixteenth century, stated that the sun was at the centre of the solar system and all the planets go around it in circles. But Copernicus was terrified that the church, which controlled nearly everything back then, would punish him for these ideas that went against what the church believed. Besides, what if he was wrong? So Copernicus published his findings only on his deathbed.

His work created waves. Suddenly, the retrograde motion of Mars made sense. When your vehicle overtakes a car on the road, the car looks to you like it is going backwards. Just like that, Earth and Mars are on different paths. Since Earth's path is smaller, at some point, it passes Mars, and that is when Mars seems to go backwards. And yet, some calculations did not tally with this idea of planets going around the sun in circles.

Along came Johannes Kepler. He worked with Tycho Brahe, a wealthy Danish astronomer who kept detailed and accurate records of his astronomical observations. Tycho was worried that young Kepler would outshine him. So he gave Kepler his data on Mars, thinking that it was so complicated that it would keep Kepler busy while Tycho could proceed to lay out details of the solar system and become famous.

In an ironic twist, it was Mars that pushed Kepler to stardom. To his utter surprise, the data showed Kepler that its orbit was like a flattened circle, or elliptical. Kepler published his calculations that proved that planets move in elliptical orbits (some are more elliptical than others). He said that an elliptical path means that at some times of the year, planets are closer to the sun. During this time, they move faster than when they are away from the sun.

Now, everything made sense. With these new ideas, our understanding of the universe changed completely.

DID YOU KNOW?

At the same time as Kepler lived, Galileo was hard at work too. With the telescopes at his diposal, he discovered Jupiter's moons. The fact that these moons orbit Jupiter, and not Earth, was another bit of evidence that Earth is not the centre of the universe. The church was angry. They warned him not to proceed with this line of study. But Galileo didn't listen, and published his findings. The church put him under house arrest, and that is how he spent the final years of his life.

What Goes Up, Comes Down

What goes up, comes down. We all know why. Gravity, duh!

Before the apple fell on Newton's head, what did people think of gravity? Did they even think about why everything fell to the ground, and didn't go up?

Turns out they did.

Aristotle wondered about it. But he had a strange theory. He felt that everything around us tries to move towards their 'natural place'. So, a stone falls to the ground because it wants to get to the earth. The stone and the earth are made of a similar material, see? Similarly, he said, smoke rises because smoke wants to go join the air, because they are the same kind of things! In the same way, water always flows downhill, to either join the ocean, the river or groundwater. That was his explanation.

Aristotle did realize that his theory had holes, but he tried to explain them away.

Many centuries later, Galileo studied gravity. The popular story says that to do so, he dropped objects from the Leaning Tower of Pisa. That sounds cool, but is probably not true.

Anyway, he did drop objects from high places. He noticed that when they fell, they became faster and faster. That is, they accelerated at a rate of 9.8 m per second square.

He also compared heavy objects and light objects. Aristotle had said, centuries ago, that heavy objects fall faster than light objects. After all, if you drop a ball and a feather, the ball will reach the ground first, won't it?

But Galileo didn't think so. He said that the feather fell slower because of its shape. The air is able to resist the feather as it falls and causes it to drift. If the feather is crushed and made into a tiny ball and dropped, it would fall just as fast as the ball. He said that if there had been no air, a heavy object and a light object would fall to the ground at the same time. In 1971, astronomer David Scott conducted Galileo's experiment on the moon with a hammer and a feather and proved Galileo right! The footage is available on YouTube.

Isaac Newton used Galileo's observations and built upon it. He said that every particle in the universe attracts every other particle with a force. The strength of this attraction depends on the masses of the two particles and how far apart they are.

Through this, Newton explained why objects fall to the earth. Attraction! He was also able to explain why planets and other celestial objects move as they do, and why they orbit around each other—they are all experiencing forces pulling them towards each other.

This is the theory of gravitation.

Einstein came along later with a newer theory that was mind-bogglingly difficult for most people to understand, but fascinating. But that's another story. But for now, on Earth, we can mostly get by using Newton's theory.

What is important is that Galileo was the first person we know who did experiments, noted down data and analysed them before coming up with a theory. And even after forming the theory, he devised tests to verify it. He made sure to check if mathematics agreed with it. It is no surprise that he is often called the father of modern science. We owe a lot to him!

DID YOU KNOW?

Did Newton really get the idea of gravity when he sat under an apple tree and an apple bopped him on the head? William Stukeley, an archaeologist, wrote a biography of Newton in which he says that Newton had told him that 'the notion of gravitation came into his mind. It was occasion'd by the fall of an apple, as he sat in contemplative mood. Why should that apple always descend perpendicularly to the ground, thought he to himself . . .'

So, there you go, the story is partially true. Maybe the apple did not directly smack him on the noggin, but it is more fun to imagine it that way!

All about Bending—Space, Time and Your Mind

Albert Einstein proposed a different explanation for gravity. Gravity is not really a pull, he said. Gravity is a result of the bending, or warping, of space and time.

Say what?

Imagine space as fabric, like your bath towel. Your friends hold out the bath towel, flat and stretched out. Now place a heavy football right in the middle of the towel. The cloth sags where the ball is. But if you sit on the ceiling fan and look down at the towel, you will still think the towel is flat. You wouldn't be able to tell that it is curved.

You can think of space as fabric too, and celestial objects, like Earth and the sun, as the football. These objects cause the fabric to curve, and it is called warping. Gravitational 'attraction' occurs due to warping. In the case of the towel, what would happen if a small marble is placed somewhere on the towel when the football is already sitting in the middle? The marble would roll towards the ball, wouldn't it? Bingo!

Similarly, when a small object is placed in a spot where space is warped because of a large object like Earth, it would move—so as to fall into the hollow created by Earth. According to Newton, when an apple falls, it accelerates to the ground. According to Einstein, it just looks that way to us.

Einstein also brought time into the picture, and said that space and time were woven together like fabric, and he called it spacetime. Earth is causing a deep hollow in spacetime, and the apple on a tree has no choice but to move through this spacetime to reach the hollow.

If this applied to all the heavenly objects, why isn't Earth falling into the hollow created by the sun, which is heavier? Thankfully, the Earth is moving too fast to fall into the arms of the sun anytime soon!

So, Einstein's ideas meant that even light bent when moving past heavy objects the size of planets and stars.

Consider a star right next to the sun in the sky. Of course, the star is far away from the sun, but from our point of view, they are next to each other. The light from this star is getting bent too. So, the star will appear to us to be at a certain position in the sky, but that is not where it actually is!

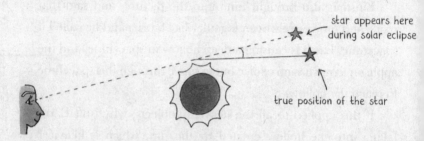

star appears here during solar eclipse

true position of the star

But how could this be confirmed? We can't even see that star when the sun is shining brightly!

There was only one way, and one time that we could take this measurement—during a total solar eclipse! The sun would be completely covered by the moon. For a few minutes, there will be enough darkness for us to be able to see the stars around the sun. We can take photographs of the position of the stars during the eclipse, and then compare them with the known position of the same stars in the sky when the sun is not around.

A young German astronomer, Erwin Finlay-Freundlich, raised money and went to Ukraine, armed with telescopes and cameras, to try and take pictures during the total solar eclipse in 1914. But war broke out, and the Russians captured him and took away his instruments.

Astronomers from California's Lick Observatory tried to capture photographs from near Kiev, but clouds played party poopers.

Meanwhile, in England, Sir Arthur Eddington, together with Astronomer Royal Sir Frank Watson Dyson, decided to try photographing the next eclipse, coming up in 1919.

Eddington went to Principe, an island off the coast of West Africa. Dyson went to Sobral in Brazil, just to make sure that if one failed, the other would succeed.

On the day of the eclipse, thunderstorms greeted Eddington. But he managed to get two photographs. Dyson had better weather, but his telescope failed him. Thankfully, he could get some pictures through a small backup telescope lent to him by a priest.

The photographs proved it. Not only did the stars appear to have shifted from their usual place, the amount of shift agreed with Einstein's calculations.

Einstein shot into fame and became the most famous scientist ever—he still is!

DID YOU KNOW?

The planet is not a perfect sphere. Its mass is not distributed evenly. So gravity is not the same everywhere on earth.

Scientists have still not completely understood gravity!

Is Air Something or Nothing?

Put a straw into a glass of water. Some of the water enters the straw at the bottom. If you suck the top of the straw, water reaches your mouth. What exactly is happening? When you suck the straw, you pull out the air that's in it. Water flows upwards, trying to fill the space left behind by the air that you have sucked out. But that is not all. You are also getting some help from air pressure. Air presses down on the water in the glass (but outside the straw). This also helps the water flow upwards inside the straw, to your mouth.

But if you had a really, really, really long straw, there would come a point where the water would stop moving, unable to reach your lips, no matter how hard you sucked the straw. The air pressure is not strong enough to push water up that high.

But we didn't know all this until recently. In the seventeenth century, Ferdinand II, the Grand Duke of Tuscany employed engineers to pump up underground water for his gardens. Try as they might, they couldn't get the water to rise beyond 10 m high—the water did not reach the surface. The Duke called the smartest guy he knew, Galileo (Yes, him again!), and asked him to figure out this problem. Galileo passed the problem on to his student, Evangelista Torricelli.

Torricelli filled a test tube with mercury up to the brim, and closed the mouth of the test tube with his finger. Then he turned it upside down with its mouth in a bowl of mercury, and slid his finger away. Some of the mercury ran out of the test tube and left a vacuum at the top of the tube.

Why didn't all the mercury flow out of the test tube, though? Torricelli correctly concluded that air was pressing down on the mercury in the bowl. At first, the mercury's own weight causes it to flow out of the test tube. But a point is reached at which the mercury's weight is the same as the pressure of air on the mercury in the bowl, and mercury stops flowing out. This shows us that air also has weight. An 'ocean of air' is pressing down upon us all, said Torricelli. This is atmospheric pressure or air pressure.

vacuum

Torricelli observed the tube every day. The level of mercury went up and down over the course of a few days. Once again, he concluded correctly that air pressure is not constant, but varies each day. He had just invented the first baroscope—an instrument that indicates variation in air pressure. This was later developed into a barometer that could actually measure atmospheric pressure.

On hearing about this, French philosopher Blaise Pascal wondered if the air pressure is different up on a mountain, compared to that near the sea. After all, there would be a smaller column of air pressing down on us on top of a mountain. Since Pascal was feeling under the weather, he sent his brother-in-law up a mountain to measure the air pressure. Those measurements proved Pascal right. There is more air weighing down on us at sea level, and so the air pressure is more, compared to the top of a mountain.

The German physicist Otto von Guericke, who was known for his theatrics, demonstrated air pressure in a way that nobody would ever forget. He even invited Emperor Ferdinand III of Austria to the demonstration.

Guericke made two huge copper hemispheres. They fit together and made a tight sphere. Guericke pulled the hemispheres in and out to show how easily they came apart.

He then put them together tightly, and using an air pump, he removed all the air from inside the sphere. Then he tied two horses to opposite sides of the sphere and made them pull hard. The hemispheres did not come apart.

He added two more horses on either side, and then two more, and two more—and still the sphere stuck together no

matter how much the horses pulled. Finally, it was only when he had eight horses on each side did the hemispheres come apart.

So, what was holding them together? The air pressure pressing down on the sphere from all sides!

DID YOU KNOW?

Robert Boyle discovered that when you increase the air pressure in a container, the volume of air decreases. This is called Boyle's law. He was also the first to predict weather using a barometer Meteorologists, scientists who study weather, can predict rain, snow, winds, tornadoes and hurricanes, and issue warnings—all by checking air pressure measurements on a barometer (with a little help from the temperature, velocity and direction of wind, along with data from previous years)!

Why did Torricelli use mercury for his measurements? Why not water? At sea level, the column of mercury in a tube will rise about 760 mm. On the other hand, a column of water at sea level would be about 10 m high! Mercury is fourteen times denser than water. Besides, it is the heaviest substance, that we know of, that stays a liquid even at ordinary temperatures. So, the barometer can stay a manageable size.

Mapping Our Way Forward

EVOLUTION OF MAPS

We depend on maps a great deal. Our faith in the GPS is so unwavering that we follow its instructions without thinking. You must have heard of stories of how the GPS has guided vehicles into the ocean, to the edge of a cliff, down a flight of stairs in a busy part of a city or on to railway tracks!

The oldest maps began as a reference to give us an idea of where we are and where we want to go.

A wall mural in Çatalhöyük, a Neolithic settlement in Turkey, is perhaps the earliest recorded map. Researchers say that the map shows the town and a volcano that blew up. It is about 8000 years old.

A 2500-year-old Italian map, called the Soleto map, has been found on a black terracotta ostracon (a piece of broken pottery with writing on it). From the same era, Babylonian clay tablets have been found with a circular map—Babylon at the centre with the Euphrates River, and surrounded by the ocean. These maps are not too detailed; they just give the user a sense of the world around them.

The first person known to have attempted making detailed maps was Ptolemy in the second century CE. He gathered documents with details about the locations of places, and obtained information from travellers. He devised a grid system, with latitudes and longitudes, and plotted the coordinates of nearly 10,000 towns in Europe, Africa and Asia!

The maps then were primarily used for military purposes. Research suggests that Ptolemy's maps helped in Rome's expansion. Since they now had information at their fingertips about the world beyond their borders, they were able to come up with plans and strategies to expand their empire.

In the fifteenth century, European countries sent people out to explore the world. Maps became essential, and skilled map-makers were in high demand. Explorers needed navigation charts, maps that had clear details of coastlines, islands, rivers, routes and harbours. Accurate maps were invaluable—the possessor of a good map had a military advantage. In fact, maps were so precious that pirates considered accurate sailing charts the most valuable treasures that they could loot from a ship!

In the 1500s, Belgian geographer Gerardus Mercator made what is now known as the Mercator map. He used a technique called a projection, which is used to fit the pattern of a curved surface (here, the earth) on to a flat surface (paper). The Mercator map was useful for navigation, because the path between two points could be represented by a straight line, making it easy for ships to know which direction to travel (even though the actual path was not a straight line!). This map also helped preserve the correct shape of each country and continent. The problem with this map is that as you go away from the equator, the map has to be stretched out. So, the land near the poles seem larger than they are. Look at your world map: Greenland and Africa look like they're the same size, but in reality, Greenland is thirteen times smaller than Africa! (Though other more accurate maps have been developed for other purposes, the Mercator map is still the one familiar to most of us.)

In the seventeenth and eighteenth centuries, as trading increased and industries developed, railroads had to be built to connect places and ferry people and materials. By that time, there were improvements in mathematics and measuring techniques, and they were applied to map-making for higher accuracy.

Map-makers started using the method of triangulation to measure land. They used the principles of trigonometry: In a triangle, if you know the length of one side and all the angles, you can calculate the lengths of the other two sides. Suppose you know the distance between two points. There is a third point such that the three points form a triangle. By measuring the angles of the triangle, you can calculate the distance to the third point. Using the calculated side and a new point, more distances can be calculated. In this way, a series of triangles can be plotted and the entire land can be mapped. The whole of India, and even the height of Mount Everest was measured using this method of triangulation.

Usually, science and technology get a boost during major wars, since it becomes important to apply all that we know to win the war. And so, with the world wars, aircraft technology improved, and along with it aerial photography—which led to better maps!

In the second half of the twentieth century, computers came to the aid of map-making and cartography. In the 1970s and '80s, GIS (Geographic Information System) emerged, which captures, stores and analyses geographic data. With GPS

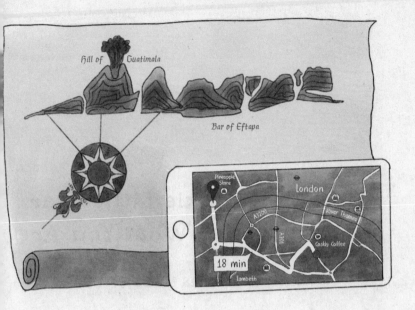

satellites, we now have eyes in space—it gives us details that we never had before. Companies like Google offer street views too, and with Google Earth, you can 'visit' any place in the world while sitting at home!

DID YOU KNOW?

Map-makers include fake towns in their maps to catch copycats! They make up a random town name, or put in a non-existent bend in a river, or a road that goes nowhere. This way, a map copycat will unknowingly copy fake features too—and get caught red-handed! The most famous fake town is Agloe, near New York. It started off as a fake town on a map, but in a strange twist, it has now turned into a real town!

Twinkle Twinkle Little Star, How I Wonder What You Are

WHAT ARE STARS MADE UP OF?

The sun and the stars are mostly made up of helium and hydrogen. But how on earth do we know this about objects millions and millions of miles away from us? It is not as if we can hop on a rocket and go find out!

We know all this because of rainbows.

A rainbow is formed when sunlight passes through droplets of water in the atmosphere. The different colours that make up sunlight bend by different amounts, enabling us to see all the colours separately. And we have a rainbow!

In the laboratory, we can split light using a prism. The colours are projected on a screen, and they form a band of colours. This is called the spectrum of that light.

The colours in the spectrum depend on the source of light. For example, the spectrum of light from an ordinary lightbulb is very different from the spectrum of light from a mercury vapour lamp.

Each element produces a unique spectrum (called the atomic spectrum)—like a fingerprint. So, we can look at the spectrum of any source of light, and we can tell what elements are present in the source.

You're getting the hang of where we are going with this, aren't you?

The same principle was used to find out what elements are in the sun and the stars. Observe the spectrum of starlight, and you will know what elements are present in that star.

But it is not entirely that simple.

A star spectrum also has narrow dark gaps where colour is missing. These gaps are called absorption lines. This is because the inside of the star emits a continuous range of colours and the elements in the star's atmosphere absorb some of these colours. This shows up as dark lines in the spectrum. What colours are absorbed depends on what elements are in the atmosphere. The absorption lines are also like signatures of these elements.

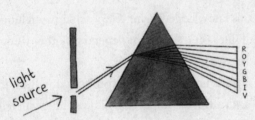

Scientists thought that if the absorption lines are wider and darker, more of that element is present in the star. With this theory, scientists concluded that the star contained nearly the same elements present on the earth—sodium, calcium, hydrogen, magnesium and iron, and in the same quantities.

Cecilia Payne-Gaposchkin was a young researcher who moved from England to the US to study. She had studied the latest theories about atomic spectra, and had also studied the work that physicist Meghnad Saha had done on the spectrum of gases at very high temperatures.

With this knowledge, Payne-Gaposchkin concluded that the thickness of lines on a spectrum depend on other things too, like temperature, density and pressure.

Also, a dark line doesn't tell you how much of an element there is in a star. But a comparison of these lines will tell you how much of each element is in a star *compared* to the other elements. She studied this thoroughly, and drew up complex tables. To cut a long story short, she arrived at the conclusion—stars have a lot of helium and hydrogen!

This was a completely weird idea at the time. Nobody believed her. She herself was doubtful, but she published her work anyway. Gradually, scientists accepted it.

Now, we know that it isn't just the sun and the stars, but most of our solar system that is made up of hydrogen and helium!

DID YOU KNOW?

Why do stars twinkle? Ha! Trick question! Stars don't twinkle. The twinkling effect is from the light of the star passing through the earth's atmosphere. When you put a spoon in water, the spoon seems to bend. This is called refraction. In the same way, the light from the stars is refracted by the gases in the earth's atmosphere. Depending on the density and temperatures of air, the intensity of the light keeps changing. This makes it look like the star is twinkling.

A spectrometer is used to spread out the light from the stars. It spreads light out much more than a normal prism does, so you can examine the colours in more detail. Scientists attach a spectrometer to a telescope and make observations and measurements.

What's the Temperature?

It's hot! Hotter than it was yesterday, but not as hot as on Friday. Last week was cooler. Not as cool as January, or maybe it was.

That's how we would talk about temperature without thermometers.

Thermometers are built on the principle that most materials expand when heated, and contract when cooled. The earliest thermometers just showed whether it was hot or cold, or whether it was hotter than yesterday or colder.

Guess what material was used in the first thermometers? Air. In 240 BCE, Philo of Byzantium connected a tube to a sphere, and put the other end of the tube into a cup of water. When it was hot, the air in the sphere expanded, and bubbled out of the other end of the tube. When it was cold, water from the cup entered the tube.

In 175 CE, Greek-born Roman physician Galen made a scaled thermometer. He took the temperature of boiling water to be the highest temperature, and ice as the coldest. A mixture of boiling water and ice was neutral, which he called zero. Then he put four points above this neutral, and four points below, and 'measured' temperatures using this basic scale.

Years later, in the seventeenth century, Galileo built a thermometer similar to Philo's equipment. At this point, it was more accurate to call it a thermoscope, because it just indicated when the temperature went up or down.

At around the same time, Italian physician Santorio Santorio made a numbered scale designed to be put into a person's mouth—the first clinical thermometer!

In 1654, Ferdinand II, Grand Duke of Tuscany, made the first sealed thermometer—he used alcohol in a tube sealed at both ends, and etched 360 marks on the tube, the number of degrees in a circle. This is probably why they started referring to temperature in degrees. Other scientists made thermometers with different scales, and substances like water and wine.

But here was the rub. Everybody used their own scales. My thermometer might have only fifteen markings, and I might say, the temperature in Mangalore is 8 today. Your thermometer might have 100 markings and you might say that the temperature in Agartala is 64 today. How do we know which place is hotter?

What they needed was a unified scale.

This is where Daniel Fahrenheit came in. Fahrenheit went to Holland as a merchant's apprentice, where he learnt about thermometers and wanted to work on them. But he was legally bound to the merchant. So, Fahrenheit ran away, dodging the Dutch police, to Denmark, Germany and Sweden, studying everywhere he went. Finally, at twenty-four, he was a legal adult, and was free to concentrate on thermometers.

Fahrenheit made the coldest substance he could: a mixture of ice, water and salts, and set it to 0—the point at which water freezes. The human body temperature was 12. This scale of 0 to

12 seemed right to him at first. But later, he realized the range was too small. He needed more numbers. So, he multiplied them all by eight. Now the freezing point of water was 32 degree F. The human body temperature became 96 degree F. (It is now considered to be 98.6.) Boiling water was 212 degree C in this Fahrenheit scale.

Fahrenheit used mercury in his thermometers. With the marketing skills he'd learnt as a merchant's apprentice, he gained famous customers and his thermometer became popular.

But as you can imagine, calculations were really hard with this scale. In the eighteenth century, a Swedish astronomer Anders Celsius came up with an easier scale, where the freezing point of water was 0 degree and boiling point was 100 degree. This was much easier to calculate with. At first, this scale was called centigrade (meaning 100 steps in Latin) but later it came to be called Celsius. Most of the world, except the US and a few other countries, have adopted the Celsius scale.

The Kelvin scale was developed in the nineteenth century by William Thomson (Lord Kelvin). Each unit is called a Kelvin, and is equal to a degree on the Celsius scale. The idea of the scale came about after scientists discovered that the volume and temperature of a gas are related. According to the theory, at a temperature of -273.15 degree C, the volume of a gas should be zero. This temperature is called absolute zero, the lowest imaginable temperature, and is the zero on the Kelvin scale. This scale is convenient because there are no negative temperatures.

DID YOU KNOW?

There are other ways to measure temperature. Some thermometers measure molecule speed (molecules of a gas move faster when the temperature of the gas increases).

Others measure infrared radiation, waves that are emitted by hot objects. The hotter the surface, the greater the radiation.

One kind measures the noise of atoms bouncing off each other. The greater the noise, the higher the temperature!

A thermistor is a resistance thermometer, whose resistance (opposition to flow of current) depends on temperature. Measure the change in resistance, and you get the temperature!

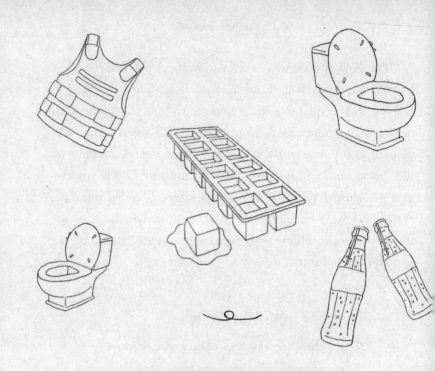

INVENTIONS

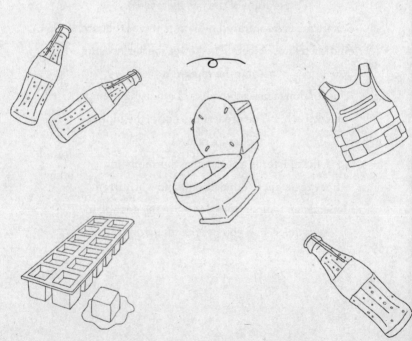

Drinking from a Straw

One sunny day in Washington DC, in 1880, Marvin Stone got himself a cool mint drink and popped a straw into it. You imagined a plastic straw, didn't you? No, this was an actual straw, a piece of rye grass, which was like a tube. But rye added an unwelcome grassy flavour to the drink. It also had the annoying habit of disintegrating into tiny pieces in the liquid. An unpleasant experience, on the whole. Could there be an alternative to a rye straw?

Straws have been around since ancient times. A seal found in a Sumerian tomb, dated 3000 BCE, show two men drinking from a jar, using long straws. Archaeologists have also found tubes made out of gold and lapis lazuli, most likely drinking straws, in the tombs. The ancient Chinese also used hollow stalks of plants to drink wine.

But why did all these people need straws in the first place? Why not drink directly from the container? Well, wine or other alcoholic drinks had sediments at the bottom of the container, and the best way to ensure they were drinking clear liquid was through a straw.

In the sixteenth century, Argentinians started using straws called *bombilla* to drink maté, a kind of tea that has leaves and other particles floating in it. The bombilla has a filter right at the bottom of the straw that ensures that only clear liquid reaches the mouth. The bombilla is still used widely.

Rye straws were popular in the US because they were cheap and easily available. But of course, they were not perfect, as was obvious to Marvin Stone. He started thinking of alternatives.

Stone took a pencil, and wrapped a long strip of paper around it. He glued the paper together, and slipped the pencil off. He now had a paper straw! But who wants glue in their drink? So, Stone made a machine that would wind paper around a tube, and then coat it with paraffin wax. This wax held the paper together, and strengthened the straw. Stone got a patent for this invention and mass produced his straws.

About fifty years later, Joseph Friedman watched his daughter trying to drink milkshake out of a paper straw. The glass was too tall for her, and the little girl tried hard to keep the glass steady as she struggled with the straight straw. She bent the straw to pull it towards her mouth, but the bend in the straw blocked the liquid. Wouldn't it be good if the straw itself was bendy?

So, Friedman inserted a screw into a paper straw. He wound dental floss around the paper over the screw, creating grooves in the straw. He removed the screw and the floss, and was left with pleats on the paper straw. This created a kind of elbow, which could now bend in any direction! He had just invented the bendy straw, and little girls could now drink their milkshakes in peace.

Guess where these bendy straws were first used? Did you guess schools? No, it was in hospitals! Patients found it easier to drink from a bendy straw while lying down.

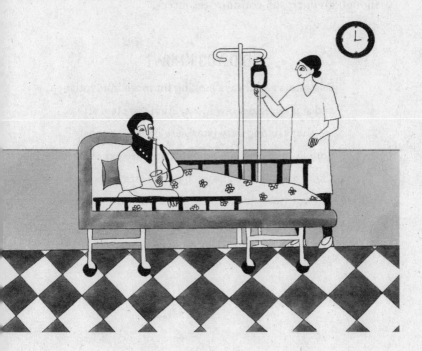

By the 1960s, paper straws were on their way out—in favour of plastic straws. They were cheap, easy to manufacture and stronger than paper straws. Since then, plastic straws have taken over the world. We are so used to straws that whether we need them or not, we reach for them.

But it has not been good for the earth. Straws are used for a very short time—just a few minutes or as long as it takes to finish our drink—but they last almost forever, polluting the earth.

We use hundreds of millions of straws every single day! A study estimates that nearly 9 billion straws (much more than the population of the earth) pollute the beaches of the world.

All over the world, governments and corporations are thinking of banning plastic straws—some cities have already enforced the ban. Many are going back to paper straws, which, though greener, still consume resources.

DID YOU KNOW?

Designers are always looking for more innovative and sustainable straw ideas. Stainless steel straws (that's a tongue twister!) are by far the most popular and practical, though they are expensive. There are silicone straws, bamboo straws, papaya stem straws, even pasta straws (imagine a long penne pasta tube), straws that you can eat, and— hold your breath—straw straws!

Bubbles Up Your Nose

SOFT, CARBONATED DRINKS

The pleasure of fizzy drinks! That tingle in your nose, that lip-smacking taste, the cool liquid trickling down your throat on a hot summer's day. Carbonated drinks are made by bubbling carbon dioxide through water, using a machine called a carbonator. But who on earth thought of bubbling carbon dioxide through water?

Nature did. Seriously. Natural springs are full of bubbles containing carbon dioxide!

Well, the first *person* to do this was probably Joseph Priestley, whom we met a few pages ago in the story about photosynthesis. For a while, Priestley lived next door to a brewery, a place where beer was produced. Fermenting beer produced a gas that hung over the beer vats like a blanket. This was carbon dioxide, which, at the time, was called mephitic air or fixed air.

When Priestley held a candle over the beer vat, the flame went out. He suspended unsuspecting mice over the vats—and they died. Let's hope they didn't fall into the beer vats!

Priestley held a container of water over the surface of the fermenting beer, and tipped it a bit, allowing the gas to bubble into the water. He tasted it; it had a pleasant, sweetish taste, and gave him a bubbly sensation in the mouth. He called the drink 'mephitic julep' and shared it with his friends. He had just become the father of fizzy drinks!

In the late 1700s in Europe, bathing in natural mineral springs was a huge fad. They also believed that drinking this natural water, which they called spa water, was good for health. But natural spa water dried up in some seasons. So, Torbern Bergman, a Swedish chemist, made a machine that used chalk and sulphuric acid to make carbonated water. He dissolved minerals into his carbonated water to make it as close as possible to natural spa water. His machine made it possible to manufacture large

quantities of this water, and now people could drink spa water through the year!

The problem with this water was that the carbonation, or fizziness, died down very soon. Then, Swiss jeweller Jacob Schweppe jumped into the fray. He made his own carbonating machine, and developed a special bottle. If you placed the bottle on its side and kept the cork moist, the contents stayed fizzy for a long time. Schweppe was able to transport and sell this water far and wide—in Geneva and in London. He added quinine to the carbonated water, and called it Schweppe's Tonic Water. It is considered the world's first soft drink and was also used as medicine. It became very popular especially with the British living in India and other parts of the British empire.

In the 1800s, there was a slew of innovations—glass bottles, bottle caps, an efficient bottling process—thanks to which bottled carbonated water was launched in a big way. Some manufacturers added flavours to it. Sodium salts were frequently added, which is why carbonated water came to be known as soda water, or soda, for short.

It was only in the late 1800s that Coca-Cola came into the picture, followed by Pepsi. Now, billions of bottles, cans and cases of soda are sold all around the world.

DID YOU KNOW?

Depending on the drink (and the country it is made in), soft drinks contain between seven and eleven teaspoons of sugar per bottle. We should rightfully call it sugar water! Tasty and inviting though it might be, it is a good idea to stay away from too much of the mephitic julep.

From Stockings to Bulletproof Vests

Glance down at one of the items you are wearing now. Did the threads or the fibres of the garment come from a plant? Or from an animal? Or did a machine make it in the factory?

How do machines make fibres, anyway? And where did this idea come from?

For centuries, we've arm-twisted nature into giving us fibres with which to make our clothes: be it plant fibres (cotton and jute) or animal-based fibres (silk and wool).

However, only the wealthier section of society has been able to afford clothes made from good quality fibres. The majority has had to make do with fibres that are uncomfortable and wear out quickly. Besides, any disaster—natural ones like flood or famine, or man-made ones like war—led to a shortage of fibres, and so, to a shortage of clothes.

People wondered, *can't we completely bypass nature and make our own fibres?*

About 150 years ago, Swiss chemist Georges Audemars dissolved the bark of the mulberry tree into a gummy rubber solution. He dipped a needle into the solution and drew it out like a thread—and made the first human-made fibre! He called it artificial silk. It later came to be known as rayon.

But Audemars's method was cumbersome. A few decades later, Englishman Sir Joseph W. Swan forced Audemars's solution through tiny holes to create long threads. This was a quicker method. His wife wove up a piece of fabric with this, and Swan displayed it at an exhibition. But it was a French chemist, Count Hilaire de Chardonnet, who started the first rayon factory and produced rayon to sell. He is known as the father of the rayon industry.

Rayon was human-made all right, but it was still derived from a tree. So, we were continuing our hunt for a fibre that we could make entirely in the factory.

In the 1930s, an American chemist Wallace Carothers, at the DuPont chemical factory, started working on finding a synthetic fibre, that is, a fibre created entirely by humans using simple chemicals. He arrived at a fibre formed by a process called condensation reaction. In this process, molecules of different chemicals combine together by a chemical reaction. This was an exciting breakthrough, but the fibre was too weak. Carothers persisted with it and realized that the water released by the reaction was falling back on the fibres that had already formed. This was preventing more fibres from being formed. He made arrangements for the water to drain out as soon as the fibre was formed. It worked!

This was a miracle fibre made entirely out of petrochemicals. It came to be called nylon.

Nylon revolutionized the world. It was cheap, elastic and could be easily produced in a factory. Unfortunately, Carothers didn't live long enough to see how his invention changed the world.

One of the first uses of nylon (apart from being used as toothbrush bristles) was to make stockings for women. Until then, stockings were made from silk, and only wealthy women could afford it. Nylon stockings did the same job at a fraction of the price! Stockings even came to be known as nylons.

During World War II, nylon production was turned entirely towards wartime use. It was used to make parachutes, ropes, tyres, tents, military uniforms and even money!

Nylon continued to be used in a great number of ways after the war—to make carpets, car seat fabric, sewing-up thread in surgery, fishing lines and pipes.

The next big invention in the fibre industry was acrylic, which was like nylon, but more wool-like. It was followed by polyester, which had an advantage over nylon—it was waterproof—and with it came an entirely new bunch of uses!

Stephanie Kwolek of DuPont (again!) was looking for a material that could replace steel wires in car tyres. She tried many combinations of polymers (materials with long chains of molecules) but none of them worked. On one of her several tries, she ended up with a solution that looked different than usual. Most polymer solutions were like thick syrup, and transparent. But this was thin, liquidy and opaque (not see-through). Kwolek could have thrown it away, but she convinced her colleague to try to make a fibre out of it anyway. Breakthrough! They ended up with a material five times stronger than steel, and much lighter too. The most important use of this material? Bulletproof vests! This material, known as Kevlar, has saved thousands of lives. It is also used in spacecraft equipment, by firefighters, in kitchen gloves, in skis, ropes, tennis racquets and car tyres among other things.

DID YOU KNOW?

Carbon Nanotube is considered to be the strongest material available now. It is a type of carbon fibre as thin as a strand of a spider's web. By itself, or combined with other materials, it has uses in engineering, aerospace, the military, in construction, renewable energy (windmill blades and fuel cells) and many more diverse fields.

When You Gotta Go, You Gotta Go

Number One and Number Two. We all do it. We've been doing it ever since life forms evolved to have digestive and excretory organs. Yet, we consider it yucky, so much so that we use euphemisms to even talk about it. It is a necessary act, but we know very little about how our ancestors emptied their bowels, probably for the same reason—it was considered too dirty and private to record. So, in many cases, we have had to study the architecture of old buildings and archaeological excavations to extract information.

What we've uncovered is that the truly disgusting part of the process is how we humans have been handling this waste over the years.

But we haven't always been so gross.

About 2500 years ago, the ancient cities of the Indus Valley Civilization had houses set in a line, and each house had private flush toilets. The waste was flushed with water and flowed out into a network of covered drains outside the home, ending up in

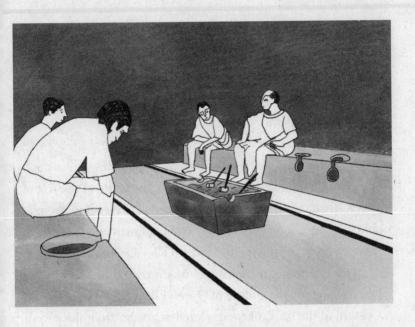

underground pits. With the fall of this civilization, their sanitary engineering knowledge was lost.

The Greeks and Egyptians had similar toilets. The community toilets of Rome had long seats with rows of holes, on which people sat next to each other and did their thing, while catching up on the latest. They wiped themselves with a sponge stuck to the end of a stick. The waste was flushed away with water.

Between 500 and 1500 CE, toilet habits reached the pits (pun intended), especially in Europe. In England, nobles peed into chamber pots placed inside their rooms. Servants emptied the contents, often out on the road. Palaces and castles had toilets that protruded out of the buildings, or chutes that led outside—and the waste simply fell out into moats or streams or rivers or into the seas! Some palaces in India, like Jaisalmer, have toilets like this. In Mughal times, the waste was sometimes just covered up with soil. As for the poor, they probably just defecated in the open—in the fields, near the rivers and in badly managed public toilets. In some cases in medieval England, they did it right inside their houses on some straw covering the floor.

These dirty practices resulted in all kinds of diseases. It led to contamination of the water supply, and thousands died of diseases like cholera.

Unbelievable? I warned you!

India had the shameful distinction of making one section of society do the dirty work of removing the waste of the rest of society, by hand. It is referred to as manual scavenging. In spite of being banned, it is still an ugly reality in many parts of India. A far cry from the days of the Indus Valley Civilization.

The first modern flush toilet was invented in 1596 by Sir John Harington, the godson of Queen Elizabeth I. His toilet had a cistern at the back, like today's toilets. Water from the cistern flowed through a pipe and flushed away the waste. But he made only two of these—one for himself and one for his godmother. It did not catch on, though.

In 1775, Alexander Cumming invented a toilet with a brilliant modification—the S-bend. Until now, the water flushed the waste directly underneath to the waste tank, and did not keep smells away. In S-bend toilets, water collected in the S-bend and created a wall of water, keeping the smells away. Though toilets have undergone more modifications after that, modern toilets (whether a squat toilet or a western-style one) use the same basic design as Cumming's S-bend.

Toilets were made of metal and wood, until, in 1885, Thomas Twyford made a porcelain version of the bowl and the pipe. That's what we use today. If you've heard that the toilet was invented by Thomas Crapper, it wasn't—in spite of his name! He was definitely involved in the business of toilets, though—he supplied toilets to the rich in the 1800s.

In the twentieth century, toilet technology really took off, with flush valves and water tanks resting on the toilet bowl itself. Many countries adopted energy laws that led to efficient toilets that made use of less water. Toilet flushing systems are also modified depending on where they need to be used. For instance, toilets on board aeroplanes use a sealed vacuum closet, where a vacuum sucks the waste out of sight.

But challenges remain. In places where there is no water even for drinking, how will people find water to flush toilets? Using recycled water for toilets is one solution. The Nano Membrane Toilet developed by Cranfield University in the UK won the Bill and Melinda Gates Foundation award for waterless toilets. The toilet separates water from human waste, and leaves behind solids that can be used as fuel. The water in the liquid waste is extracted by the process of pervaporation, where liquid is vapourized through a membrane. The vapours are collected and drained into a vessel. This water can be used for irrigation, household washing—and even drinking! The toilet works without water and electricity. Practical problems still need to be ironed out, and more research is underway.

DID YOU KNOW?

The term 'getting the wrong end of the stick' means to misunderstand or misinterpret a situation. One of the theories about the origin of this phrase is that it came from the ancient Roman toilet habits—the stick with the sponge. The right end of the stick is, of course, the one you hold. The wrong end—well, enough said about that.

Write On!

THE HISTORY OF PAPER

Paper is everywhere. Newspapers, books, tissues, paper napkins . . . You don't even have to take your eyes off this book to see paper!

Where did paper come from?

Ancient Sumerians wrote on wet clay tablets using reeds. They were too heavy and cumbersome though. Ancient Indians wrote on leaves. But leaves tended to rot away. The ancient Chinese wrote on wood (too heavy) and silk (too expensive).

People even used parchment (untanned skin of sheep, goats and calves) and vellum (skin of young animals like lambs) to write on, but they were expensive and not easily available.

Then, about 5000 years ago, the Egyptians tried something different. They cut the reeds of papyrus, a river plant, into strips, and laid them side by side. Papyrus is sticky, so the strips melded with one another and resulted in flat sheets, which they wrote on. (The word paper is derived from papyrus.) But it took too long to make and was expensive.

A Chinese court official, Ts'ai (Cai) Lun, wanted a material cheaper than silk to write on. In the first century CE, he mashed up tree bark, plants, cotton rag and even fish nets together with water. He strained the gooey mess and ended up with pulp. He flattened the pulp and dried it—and made the first sheet of paper! (Recent archaeological digs in China have discovered paper that has been dated to 200 BCE, but they don't know who made it.)

The Chinese tried to keep the art of papermaking a secret, but the knowledge spread to Korea and Japan. Soon, the Arabs learnt it, and started the first papermaking industry in Baghdad in the eighth century. Slowly, it spread to North Africa and then Europe in the twelfth century. It reached the Americas in the 1600s. (But the Mayans in the fifth century already used *amate*, similar to paper, made out of bark!)

By the 1700s, paper was used everywhere, and the demand was extremely high. But they were running out of cotton rags. People robbed Egyptian tombs to steal linen that mummies were wrapped with (and there was a lot of it—sometimes a kilometre of linen on just one mummy!). In England, they even passed a law that bodies should be buried wearing woollen garments, not cotton clothes. They wanted that cotton to make paper!

In 1719, the French scientist René Réaumur got an idea from paper wasps. These creatures chew up wood and release a kind of fine paper to make their nests. *Does that mean we could make paper out of wood too*, he wondered.

Taking off on Réaumur's idea, in the 1830s and 1840s, German Friedrich Gottlob Keller and Canadian Charles Fenerty independently invented machines that made paper out of wood pulp. Keller sold his idea to German industrialist Heinrich Voelter, who started manufacturing—not paper itself—but these wood-grinding machines for papermaking. From there, the technology spread around the world, and more innovation followed.

Today, paper is made from trees grown specially for the purpose. Paper mills also use waste wood chips, sawdust and recycled paper. With the world increasingly going online, paper consumption is reducing.

DID YOU KNOW?

Some nineteenth-century books are already disintegrating because of the chemicals used in it. But the paper nests of the paper wasps probably last forever!

In the 1400s, the Chinese used old, unwanted books to make paper. That is the first known instance of recycling paper. Today, almost 35 per cent of paper is made from recycled paper.

It's So Cool!

One of the best feelings ever is to reach for a cool drink on a hot day. What *would* we do without refrigerators? Wait. What *did* we do before refrigerators were invented?

We've used all kinds of tricks to keep things cool. Some are simple—like clay pots. They work in the same way as the human body keeps itself cool—by sweating! Our body releases a little water, which evaporates, taking along with it some of the body's heat. That is how we keep cool. In the same way, clay pots have tiny pores, and some of the water from inside the pot seeps out, evaporates and keeps the water inside cool.

Some cultures buried pots underground, or immersed closed vessels in flowing streams, or just placed them in cool, shady places. At some point, we started to depend on ice to preserve food and drink.

The first refrigerator, or rather, icebox, was probably the Persian Yakhchal, or ice pit, that was in use about 2500 years ago. Yakhchals are massive dome-shaped structures. The Persians lugged ice from the nearby mountains and stored it inside these

Yakhchals. Lucky royals got to eat cool falooda chilled by the ice from the Yakhchals.

Over the centuries, people harvested natural ice from lakes, rivers or mountains, wrapped the ice up in straw, cloth or wood and stored them underground. They could then use them as needed. But generally, cooling was used more for chilling than for preserving food. They had other ways of preserving food, like drying, fermenting and adding sugar, salt or oil.

Iceboxes started appearing in homes in the nineteenth century in the West. They looked similar to the refrigerators of today. However, they did not make their own cool air, but contained ice blocks that kept food cool. Iceboxes were made of wood, lined with tin or zinc and insulated with sawdust or seaweed. Naturally, the ice melted eventually, no matter how good the insulation. A tray underneath collected the melted water, and it was emptied frequently. Ice vendors went from door to door, selling ice blocks, like today's vegetable and fruit vendors do.

The vendors got their ice blocks from commercial ice storage houses—large buildings where blocks of ice were stored. It was an entire industry at one time. Frederic Tudor, an American businessman known as the 'Ice King', shipped ice from cold countries to hot countries. On ships. Across the oceans. Half the ice melted by the time it reached the destination, but Tudor learned how to insulate the ships better, and eventually, made sure that most of the ice reached intact.

But iceboxes were expensive and inconvenient. There had to be some other way to keep things cool.

Benjamin Franklin and chemist John Hadley studied how evaporation affects temperature. They rubbed ether on a

thermometer. When the ether evaporated, the thermometer showed a lower temperature. This way, they were able to make the temperature drop to below freezing point! Oliver Evans, another American, took these principles and tried to draw up a plan for a refrigerator. But other ideas (like the steam engine) called out to him and he got distracted.

Not to worry. Jacob Perkins, another American inventor, took this idea from Evans, developed it and got a patent for the vapour compression refrigerator. The same concept is still used in modern refrigerators. How it works: A substance (called a refrigerant) circulates through the refrigerator. It absorbs heat from inside the refrigerator and turns into vapour. The vapour is compressed in a compressor. This high pressure vapour passes through a condenser, where it cools down, and releases heat outside. The cycle repeats. Perkins is known as the father of refrigeration.

In later years, people tried to find refrigerants that were better than ether. They tried ammonia. Too smelly. They tried methyl chloride gas. Too toxic. People died. Finally, they created the compound chlorofluorocarbon or CFC (also known as freon). CFC was used in refrigerators for years—until scientists discovered that it was harming the ozone layer of the earth. So, CFC was phased out. More environmentally friendly refrigerants are being used now, like ethane, isobutane, propane and so on. Researchers are trying to find better refrigerants that are safer and more efficient.

DID YOU KNOW?

Albert Einstein worked on a design for a refrigerator. In the 1920s, Einstein read that a toxic refrigerator coolant leaked and killed all the members of a sleeping family. In anguish, he got together with his former student Leo Szilard, and they designed a refrigerator with no moving parts, so there were no seals with the potential to leak. Though they got patents for their design, there were some practical problems with it. It was abandoned in favour of other designs. But since it was a more environmentally friendly design, scientists are revisiting the design now to see if they can modify it to bring cooling solutions to countries with developing economies.

Dead Frog Dancing

HOW BATTERIES WERE INVENTED

Pass a comb through your hair, and hold the comb next to some pieces of paper. The comb attracts the paper. That happens due to static electricity. It is the same thing that causes your hair to stand up sometimes, especially in dry weather, or you feel a little spark or a shock when you touch another person. Electrons, which are negative electric charges, sometimes collect on objects. Another object can lose some of the electrons on its surface and become positively charged. If two objects have similar charges on them, the objects repel. If they have opposite charges, the two objects attract. The spark or the shock occurs when the static electricity is discharged; that is, when electrons flow from one object to another through air. Lightning is also a strong form of this kind of discharge.

Humans had observed static electricity for a long time, but did not know what exactly it was.

In the past few centuries, scientists made machines called electrostatic generators that generated electric charges. These were used in experiments.

But was there a way to store this electric charge for later use?

In the late eighteenth century, a German experimenter Ewald G. von Kleist closed an empty medicine bottle with a wooden cork, and banged a nail through the cork. He brought the nail in contact with the electrostatic generator, and then kept it aside. After a while, he touched the nail with his hand, and got a huge shock—a literal shock as well as a huge surprise! He had just discovered a way to store electrical charge.

The following year, Pieter van Musschenbroek of Leyden dipped a metal rod half into a jar of water. He then brought the top of the rod in contact with the electrostatic generator. When he touched the rod later, he got such a violent shock that he thought he was done for. This came to be known as the Leyden jar.

A Leyden jar was compact and mobile. So, scientists could easily charge it and carry it around. They needn't be in the same room as the electrostatic generator any longer! However, the Leyden jar discharged all at once. Capacitors, important components used in electrical devices, are like Leyden jars, so these have their uses too, but scientists were looking for a gadget that would store charges and discharge them slowly. Inspiration for that came from . . . frogs. Luigi Galvani, an Italian physicist, was experimenting with frogs' legs. Just the legs; no head. During a storm, he touched a frog's nerves with a pair of metal scissors. The frog's legs twitched. He tried the same thing when there was no storm, but when an electrostatic generator was on in the room, and he got the same result.

Was it the storm or the electrostatic generator causing this weird movement of the legs? To answer his own questions, he tried touching the frog's nerves with two metal pieces, when there was no storm, and when the electrostatic generator was turned off. The frog still danced.

Galvani was delighted. He concluded that animals generate their own electricity, and called it animal electricity. He even thought that he had reanimated the dead frog. Naturally, this idea excited a lot of people. Mary Shelley wrote the novel *Frankenstein* inspired by this concept.

Even now, the word galvanize is used for when someone is encouraged or inspired into action!

Galvani was both right and wrong. We now know that most of the human body's processes depend on electrical impulses, so he had the right idea about that. But he was not right about the body actually producing electricity the way he thought it did. We'll see why in a moment.

However, Galvani's experiments galvanized (see what I did there?) another Italian physicist, Alessandro Volta, to do experiments of his own. Volta got the same results as Galvani. But Volta concluded that the frog's leg did indeed twitch because of electricity—but this electricity didn't come from within the

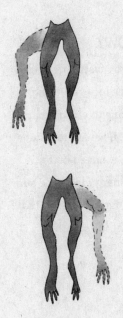
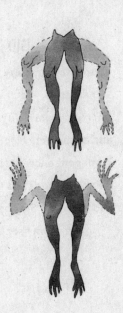

frog. An electric current was produced because of the contact between two different metals (the metal probe and the brass hook that fixed the frog's leg to the board) in a moist environment (the frog's leg.)

Taking this idea further, Volta placed discs of zinc and copper alternately in a box. Between these discs, he placed pieces of cardboard soaked in salt solutions. Then he connected wires to the discs at the two ends, and joined the wires, completing the circuit. An electrical current was produced! By increasing or decreasing the number of discs and the connecting fluid (called electrolyte), Volta could control how much electric current was produced.

He had created the first reliable source of electric power. It was called the voltaic pile, and is considered the first battery. It immediately galvanized (forgive me!) other scientists all over the world to use it for their own experiments, or try and make better ones for different purposes.

DID YOU KNOW?

Battery technology is one of the fastest growing industries. We need batteries for everything, starting from a tiny smartphone to electric cars and even home electrification. If we are to reduce dependence on fossil fuels, we need better, reliable batteries to store the energy from the sun and the wind. Soon, we should have batteries that charge in seconds, but last for months.

Seeing Clearly

Statistics suggest that more than half the humans in the world wear or need glasses. That's every second person who needs some kind of vision correction!

In earlier centuries, people used marbles, or naturally occurring glass, or even glass containers filled with water to magnify objects to see clearly.

It is said that Nero, emperor of Rome, watched sports and games through an emerald. Some versions say that the emerald was hollowed out and acted as a lens through which he could see better. But other versions say that he just used it as an anti-glare device.

In the 1200s, Italian craftspeople moulded rock crystal into convex shapes. Convex crystals made objects appear bigger. Scholars used these shaped crystals to study texts, and craftsmen could work on intricate craft. They placed these lenses over the text or on the objects themselves, or else, they held them in their hands, close to the eye. But grubby fingers smudged lenses!

In the 1300s, Italians made the first eyeglasses. They fixed metal or leather rims to two convex lenses and attached them side by side. A handle was attached to this set-up. Scholars and craftspeople used the handle to position the two lenses in front of their eyes to see. However, one hand was always occupied with the glasses, and besides, the hand had to be steady, which wasn't always possible.

Eventually, in later designs, they bent the connecting bridge between the two lenses into a curve or a hook and placed it on their nose, but it still wasn't quite efficient—it kept sliding down the nose.

In the 1400s, the printing press was invented, books flooded the market and the demand for eyeglasses shot up. More people started working on perfecting eyeglasses. The rims or frames were now made of whalebone, horn and tortoiseshell. They also became more inventive in thinking up ways to make sure the glasses stayed on the nose and didn't slide down, so that you could have your hands free to concentrate on what you wanted to do. They put in a little spring at the bridge, which would pinch the nose and keep the glasses steady. It was annoying and painful, but it did the job. This type of glasses were called pince-nez—French for pinch-nose!

The 1600s saw improvement in both glass technology as well as metal work. Metal made it easier to shape the bridge better, so that it settled snugly on the nose. They also tried other ways to ensure that the glasses didn't fall off. They connected ribbons to the lenses and tied them around the head, or looped them around the ears, or used a bar under their wigs, connected to the glasses, to make it sit tight on the nose.

At around this time, Spanish notary Benito Daza de Valdés made a systematic study of lenses for the first time. He determined how much corrective power each lens had, and how to choose lenses. He put all the data into tables. He placed little black mustard seeds in rows, and asked people to count the seeds, standing at increasingly greater distances. He noted the distance at which people could no longer count the seeds, checked his tables and told them what power lenses they would need to use for clear vision. This was the first time anybody had systematically tabulated corrective lenses like this.

In the 1700s, 'temple glasses' were introduced, with long stems or arms (called temples) that connected the frame of the lenses to the back of the ear. Modern glasses are versions of that design.

At around the same time, Benjamin Franklin invented the bifocals. He was both short-sighted as well as long-sighted, and needed one set of glasses for reading and another for looking at distant things. He was tired of switching between glasses. So, he attached the two lenses together and wore a single pair of eyeglasses.

In the eighteenth century, the rich used eyeglasses like items of jewellery. Different designs, like monocles (with only one lens), lorgnettes (like opera glasses, with a handle) were made with gold and studded with precious jewels to show off their class and wealth!

With the invention of plastics and clearer lenses in the nineteenth century, glasses became lighter and better. By rights, we should now be calling them 'eye-plastics'! Even though contact lens and vision corrective surgeries are now common, eyeglasses are still popular and in fashion.

DID YOU KNOW?

British professor Joshua Silver has invented self-adjusting glasses. The lenses are made up of flexible membranes filled with silicone oil. There are adjustable syringes on the side of the lenses, using which, you can increase or decrease the amount of oil inside the membrane, and thus change the power of the glasses to what you need. The advantage of this is that a bunch of these generic glasses can be shipped anywhere, even to remote areas—and at the end point, it can be corrected on the spot to suit the person who needs it. It is much cheaper than to make glasses of a specific power and then ship them.

Colour Me Happy

HISTORY OF CRAYONS

The next time adults around you feign annoyance about how, when you were a toddler, you would grab crayons with your chubby fingers and make 'art' on the walls, you can tell them you were just doing what Palaeolithic people did!

Okay, Palaeolithic people didn't have crayons, but the painting techniques they used were similar to how crayons work.

They mixed coloured mud and soot with animal fat to draw images in their caves. Grease, or fat, helps fix the colours to the surface you apply colours on. They also last for a long time. (Many Palaeolithic paintings are still intact on cave walls in Europe.)

This principle was used by the ancient Greeks and Egyptians too. They mixed beeswax and colours, heated the mixture and then quickly applied it to the base—stone or wood—before it dried. These paintings are called encaustic paintings.

In modern times, we know that Leonardo da Vinci used wax-based coloured sticks for his art. He also probably made his own crayons—after all, many artists made their own crayons at the time.

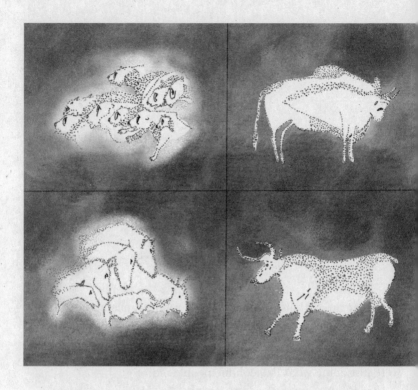

The term crayon itself was first used in the 1600s, and came from the words 'craie' (French for chalk) and 'creta' (Latin for clay). If you are wondering why we are talking about chalk when we were just talking about wax and colours, well, the first few colouring sticks were made out of chalk. The next step was what were called pastels—pigment powder rolled tightly into sticks with a binder. These were hard in structure.

The conté crayon, developed by French scientist Nicolas-Jacques Conté, came next. Conté combined clay and graphite and made crayons in black, red and brown colours.

We are not sure who made the first wax crayons as we know them, but it is likely that it was a French manufacturer Joseph Lemercier. At the time though, beeswax was the main material used, and it was hard and expensive.

As manufacturing techniques grew in the 1800s, new materials came into use in industry. Paraffin, a material derived from petroleum, was one of them. European manufacturers started using paraffin to make wax crayons. It is paraffin that is used most widely in crayons today. This was a huge breakthrough in crayon making and turned out to be very popular, especially because the marks made by these crayons could not be erased by rubbing, by acids, or by water.

Soon, American manufacturers borrowed the ideas and they entered crayon manufacturing too. One of them, Charles Bowley, made paraffin crayons in the shape of pencils for the first time, put them in a box and sold them.

Another development coincided with its manufacturing—the start of early education for children. Until now, crayons were used mostly by artists and industries. But this was a new market! As new schools came up and education for children began to be recognized as a priority, lots of people jumped in to make crayons for children.

Crayons were easy to hold, easy to store. There was no worry about spilling, there was no worry about staining clothes. It was perfect!

Or was it?

There actually was a huge problem that made itself known pretty soon. Children tend to put things into their mouths. And these crayons weren't exactly safe. So, manufacturers had to adapt quickly. They started to use non-toxic pigments that would be safe even if they were swallowed.

Around this time, Edwin Binney and C. Harold Smith got into crayon making. They already owned a business in which they manufactured pigment to make tyres black—to increase their strength—and red oxide of iron for painting barns.

They also made lampblack and dustless chalk. They brought out colourful crayons under the brand name Crayola, which caught on in America. (Many Americans even now say Crayola when they mean crayons.)

After that, it was only a matter of time before it spread all across the world, making it one of the most popular stationery items for children in the world.

DID YOU KNOW?

Crayola had a colour called 'Flesh', which was peach coloured. It was meant for colouring in the skin part of drawings of human beings. But it also implied that there were no other skin colours. In the 1960s, when black people in America were fighting for their civil rights, Crayola quietly changed the name of the colour to 'peach'. Even in India, the problem exists. Six years ago, a lawyer noticed that one of the crayon sets available in India has a colour labelled 'skin' which was peach in colour, and it is ridiculous because a majority of Indians have naturally brown skin tones. So, he sued the company. The case is ongoing, but another crayon company in India took the hint and changed the name of their 'skin' crayon to 'peach'.

Wiping It Clean

THE HISTORY OF ERASERS

What would we do without erasers? Imagine how hesitant we would be to make a mistake if we didn't have an eraser (or a delete key!).

The ancient Sumerians did not need erasers. They used clay tablets, which were forgiving of mistakes. All they had to do was smooth out mistakes on the soft clay with their fingers before the clay dried. The Greeks and Romans wrote on animal skin, particularly baby animals' skin, such as the skins of lamb, calf or goat kid. They were expensive, so they used to scrape off the writing and then reuse the skin. Animal skin with the writing scraped off was called palimpsest. Papyrus, made out of the pulp of papyrus plants, was washed to get rid of marks, or was rubbed with stone.

An eraser to remove graphite marks, that is, marks made by a pencil lead, became necessary only with the invention of pencils. Pencils came into existence in the sixteenth century, when people wrapped graphite in string and cloth and leaves (to avoid blackening their fingers) and then wrote with them.

The first object they used to erase pencil marks was—bread. They moistened bread, balled it up and used it as an eraser. I know you're itching to try it out and see if it works. Go ahead. I'll wait.

Bread was cheap and easily available, but it was, well, bread. It went bad. It developed fungus.

Then, French scientist and explorer Charles-Marie de La Condamine brought back from his travels a gummy substance called India rubber. The South American tribes used it as an adhesive. Joseph Priestley popularized it as a good way to rub out graphite marks, and called it rubber.

Edward Nairne was the first to market these blobs of gum.

However, rubber was, after all, a plant product. It rotted and stank after some time. Its quality changed with the weather and it crumbled when used.

In the nineteenth century, Charles Goodyear treated natural rubber with sulphur, a process called vulcanization. This made rubber hard, and it didn't spoil. Vulcanized rubber turned out to be great for tyres and erasers!

Modern erasers are made with a combination of plastic, vinyl, synthetic rubber or some kind of gum. Electric erasers, used in art and for technical drawing, use lesser pressure, are gentler on the paper and can erase small, targeted parts.

Erasing ink was a bigger challenge. Some ink erasers make the writing invisible through a chemical reaction, so that it can be written over. Correction fluids—thin white paint applied with a brush over an error, and then written over—are also commonly used.

Now computers have convenient delete and backspace keys. The spellcheck option ensures your writing ends up mistake-free (well, almost). Autocorrect rectifies most errors on smartphones and computers even as we type—and we end up never knowing the correct spelling of some words!

DID YOU KNOW?

When we write with a pencil, the graphite mixes with the fibres of the paper. The molecules that make up erasers are stickier than the molecules of paper. So, when we run an eraser on pencil marks, graphite particles end up sticking to the eraser, almost like a magnet, or a vacuum cleaner!

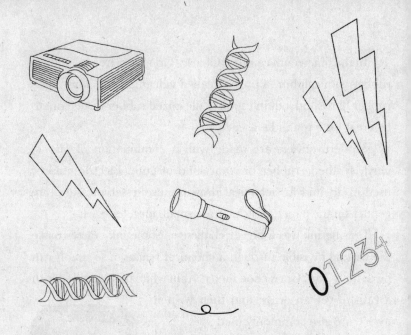

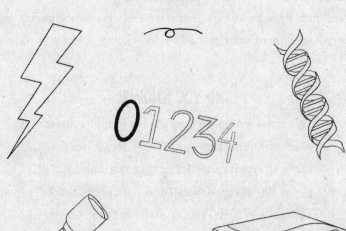

IDEAS THAT CHANGED
THE WORLD

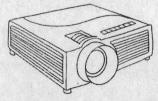

All the Light We Cannot See

ULTRAVIOLET AND INFRARED LIGHT

Clever though we might be, humans have really poor eyesight. Don't start munching on those carrots now; not much use in this case. It's just that our eyes don't have the ability to see all the colours that are out there in nature.

Sunlight is made up of seven colours that we can see. But it also contains light that we cannot see—infrared and ultraviolet light. On the other hand, 'lowly' creatures like insects can see these colours. Some flowers might look ordinary to us, but to insects and some birds, these flowers look magnificent and glittery, as if sprinkled with fairy dust. So, bees make, well, a beeline to these flowers.

If we humans can't see those colours, how did we discover that these colours exist?

Frederick William Herschel, a German-born British astronomer, wanted to measure the temperature of light. In the year 1800, he shone a beam of light on to a prism. The prism split the light into a spectrum of seven different colours. He let the coloured light fall on different thermometers. The thermometer

readings showed him that blue light was hotter than violet light, green light was hotter than blue, and so on. Red light was the hottest of them all. At this point, he could have wrapped up the experiment and gone home. But a scientist is always curious. On a whim, he placed a thermometer beyond the red light, where there was no light at all, as far as he could see. To his astonishment, the reading on the thermometer was much higher at this point! There *was* light there—only we could not see it.

He had just discovered infrared light (infra—below). It was the first time that anybody had proven that there was light beyond what we can see.

Johann Ritter, a German chemist and physicist, heard about this experiment, and in 1801, wondered if there could be a similar invisible light on the other side of the spectrum, beyond violet. Measuring the temperature at that point wouldn't work as the temperature rise would be too small to be measured reliably. So, Ritter had to find another way. He used silver chloride, which, when exposed to sunlight, tarnished and turned black. Like Herschel, Ritter also used a prism to split light into a spectrum and directed the different coloured light on to strips of silver chloride. Red light tarnished the strip slightly, the orange and yellow a little more, and so on. The blue and violet lights tarnished the strip considerably. Then he placed a strip beyond the violet light, where there was no visible light. To his satisfaction, he observed that the strip tarnished more dramatically at this point than with any other colour! This confirmed his suspicion that there is light beyond violet. This was ultraviolet light (ultra—beyond).

We can't see this light, but so what? We've found uses for them anyway. Ultraviolet rays are used in astronomy, lighting and in medicine for sterilization and disinfection. Infrared rays are used to treat skin diseases and relieve soreness. Hot objects

give out infrared radiation, so we can use it to 'see' objects even in the dark, and we can measure this radiation to know how hot the object is. So infrared radiation finds uses in medicine (thermometers), astronomy, communication and in the military.

DID YOU KNOW?

The lens in our eye filters out UV light. Evidence shows that some people are able to see a little of the UV light once the lenses in their eyes are removed during cataract surgery. UV light is bluish, and so they see things as bluer than we do. The painter Claude Monet started painting bluish paintings after his cataract surgery—most likely, he saw more of blue and was just painting what he saw!

The Fastest Thing Ever

SPEED OF LIGHT

How fast does light travel? Infinitely fast, thought the ancient philosophers Aristotle and Descartes; light just goes from the source to the destination instantly. This was the general belief until about 400 years ago.

Galileo Galilee (yet again!) was one of the first scientists to think of measuring the speed of light. His method involved him and his assistant standing on two hills some distance away from each other. Galileo flashed a light from his lantern, and the assistant answered by flashing his light as soon as he saw the light from Galileo's lantern. Galileo tried to measure how long it took between the time he flashed his light and he saw the assistant's flash. No matter how far apart he and his assistant stood, Galileo wasn't able to record the time.

A few decades later, twenty-one-year-old Danish astronomer Ole Roemer went to the Paris observatory to work under the world-famous astronomer Jean-Dominique Cassini. Cassini was an authority on planets, satellites and their orbits.

However, Cassini had been puzzling over the behaviour of Io, one of Jupiter's moons. Io, of course, orbits Jupiter. In each orbit, Jupiter eclipses Io once (as seen from Earth). It appeared that the time between two Io eclipses wasn't constant. Sometimes, the next Io eclipse happened very quickly. At other times, the time interval between two Io eclipses was longer.

Cassini wondered why. Maybe Io moves in a weird way or wobbles? Perhaps it has a strange orbit?

But young Ole Roemer turned the problem on its head. What if it isn't a question of how Io moves? What if it was related to how Earth moves? As he studied the data, an astonishing fact jumped out at him. When Earth was near Jupiter, lesser time passed between two Io eclipses. When Earth was at the other end of the solar system, far away from Jupiter, more time passed between two Io eclipses.

Roemer had a flash of insight. What if the eclipses are occurring at equal intervals of time, but we are just *seeing* the eclipse later when we are far away from Jupiter? If this was true, this could only mean one thing—light from Io and Jupiter takes extra time to reach us when we are far away. That means light must have a certain speed.

From his observations, Roemer calculated that it must take 22 minutes for light to travel from one end of the Earth's orbit to the other end. The diameter of the Earth's orbit was already known. So, the speed of light could be determined with this formula:

$$\text{Speed of light} = \frac{\text{(Diameter of Earth's orbit)}}{\text{(Time taken for light to cover the distance)}}$$

Dutch scientist Christiaan Huygens did the calculations and arrived at 1,31,000 miles per second. It was amazing that they arrived at this approximate value back then, when measuring instruments were not that sophisticated. The actual speed as we now know is 1,86,000 miles per second.

Cassini's supporters didn't believe Roemer's results. Poor Roemer was shamed and forced to go back to Denmark. It was only fifty years later that other scientists proved him right.

In the 1800s, Hippolyte Fizeau and Léon Foucault separately tried to find out a more accurate speed of light. Their idea was the same as Galileo's, but the contraptions they used were more sophisticated. Fizeau sent a beam of light through a gap in a rotating wheel. A mirror some distance away reflected the beam of light and sent it back towards the wheel. He adjusted the speed of the wheel so that the reflected beam came back through the next gap in the wheel. Knowing the speed of the wheel, and the distance to the mirror, they could calculate the time. Foucault's set-up was similar. Both of them got pretty accurate results.

But it was Albert Abraham Michelson who got the most accurate results of all. He tried Galileo's idea at first. He set up a light on Mount Wilson Observatory in California, and one on a mountain 22 miles away, but he realized that wind and atmospheric conditions might affect his results.

What if he conducted the experiment in a huge, mile-long steel pipe without air to disturb the light? But municipal officials did not help him get such a pipe. So, he decided to make one himself. In 1931, he fixed together 60-foot pipes and sealed them with rope, canvas, tape, glue and the inner tubes of tyres. He propped it on tottering wooden props. It didn't look like much, but it served his purpose, especially after he reduced air pressure in it. He used the same principles as Fizeau and Foucault. A beam bounced off one face of a rotating sixteen-sided mirror, was reflected back from the other side of the pipe and came back and hit the next face of the sixteen-sided mirror. With this, he got the figure 1,86,271 miles per second. It is very nearly what we now accept as the speed of light.

DID YOU KNOW?

The speed of light seems very large. It feels like it is impossible to make an object move at that speed. But the Large Hadron Collider in CERN, Switzerland, pushes atomic particles at nearly the speed of light through a tunnel, before they are made to collide. It aims to answer questions about our universe and its origin. It has already given us several answers and is expected to provide many more.

Catching Criminals
with Science

More than 2000 years ago, a local ruler in Greece gave a goldsmith a lump of gold and ordered him to make a pure gold crown out of it. After the crown was ready, the ruler became suspicious. Had the goldsmith kept a part of the gold for himself? Had he used silver to make up for the gold he had stolen? The ruler summoned Archimedes of Syracuse and asked him to find out if the goldsmith had been honest—without destroying the crown.

While still mulling over the problem, Archimedes went to take his bath. As he lowered himself into the bathtub, the water level rose. The more he immersed himself, the higher the water rose. Suddenly, he shot up in a splash of water and ran through the streets naked, shouting 'Eureka!' (I've got it!) That's how the story goes.

What was it that he got? The solution of course. When an object is immersed in water, it displaces some water. The volume

of this water is equal to the volume of the object. Silver is less dense than gold. A lump of 1 kg of silver would be larger than a lump of 1 kg of gold. So, a crown that had both gold and silver in it would displace more water than a crown of pure gold (of the same weight)! Archimedes applied this idea to the crown, and the goldsmith ended up in prison.

This was probably one of the first instances where science was used to solve a crime. Forensic science applies science and technology to catch criminals.

Way back in 1247 in China, Song Ci wrote *The Washing Away of Wrongs*, the first forensic book. He talked about poisoning, wounds, fake wounds, how to differentiate between different kinds of deaths, and many other topics of interest to the police. He also described in detail how to examine a dead person, and find out when the person died—details necessary for crime-solving. This book sold well, and was translated into many languages. A few decades later, influenced by Song Ci's book, a magistrate in Italy ordered an autopsy (examination of a dead body) legally for the first time. Bartolomeo da Varignana, a doctor, performed the autopsy to check if there was anything suspicious about the death.

With the invention of the microscope in the sixteenth century, another channel of investigation opened up. Investigators could now study tiny hair, fibres, wounds, glass, and of course, blood.

Until the 1800s, arsenic was a popular poison used by murderers to kill people, because it showed no obvious signs of having affected the person. Most people assumed the victim died from bad health, and the murderer walked free. Until chemistry came to the rescue. A man was suspected of murdering his grandfather. The police called in a British chemist, James Marsh, to investigate. Marsh devised a sensitive test to check for arsenic, and tested the stomach lining of the dead man. He did find arsenic, and the grandson was found guilty of murder! As an immediate result of the Marsh test, cases of arsenic poisoning dropped dramatically.

Eventually, guns became popular as murder weapons. Scotland Yard (the headquarters of the London Metropolitan Police) studied bullets, and discovered that bullets acquire tiny marks depending on the gun from which they are fired. Using this, they could figure out which bullet came from which gun, and that way, they could catch the killer.

Any improvement in technology leads to improvement in other unrelated fields. Photography turned out to be a blessing for crime solvers! Photographs of criminals were stored in files. Photos could now be published in newspapers and on posters, requesting information on wanted criminals. A

French policeman, Alphonse Bertillon, studied angles, lighting and measurements in photography, and made significant improvements in photography for forensic use.

Fingerprints, meanwhile, had been used for a long time to keep records. It was known that it was unlikely for two people to have the same fingerprints. In the late 1800s, Francis Galton calculated that the chances of two people having the same fingerprints was one in 64 billion. At around the same time, a murder was solved in Argentina, using fingerprint matching.

In the early 1900s, two Indians, Azizul Haque and Hem Chandra Bose, created a system of fingerprint classification, still used under the name Henry classification system. The first fingerprint bureau was set up in Calcutta.

But the true revolution came with the discovery of DNA analysis—that everybody has a unique biological code. DNA has revolutionized forensic science. Samples of hair, skin,

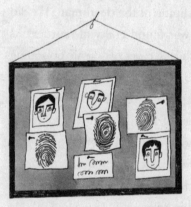

blood and other bodily fluids found on the victim or on the crime scene can be matched to criminals. Old unsolved cases can be pulled out, and criminals can be convicted by comparing their DNA with old DNA evidence. Innocent people who were wrongly imprisoned have also been released, thanks to DNA evidence.

The advent of computers has also changed the game. Computers are used to create graphics, sketches of suspects and simulations, making it easier to visualize the crime scene. It also makes everything faster, like searching records for information.

Other advanced technology, like electron microscopes, UV and infrared light testing, chemical analysis techniques, eye scans, voice fingerprinting have all helped catch criminals. It's getting increasingly harder to get away with being a bad guy!

DID YOU KNOW?

People upload their DNA on genealogy websites (to find their family tree or genetic ancestry). In cases where the police have a suspect's DNA, but have lost track of the suspect himself, the police can go through these records on the website, look for a match for the DNA they have on file. Even if they find DNA belonging to a relative of the suspect, they can track down the suspect through the relative. Using this strategy, the US police have cracked a number of old, unsolved cases.

The Relationship That Ushered in a New Era

ELECTROMAGNETISM

Imagine this: You are attending a lecture by a scientist in an auditorium. The scientist makes a discovery onstage. Not just any discovery—but one that is going to change our world. And yet, you yawn, unaware that you are witnessing a historic moment.

It was the early 1800s and there had been exciting developments in science. Benjamin Franklin had conducted an experiment half a century previously to show that lightning is a form of electricity.

Magnets had been known to humans for a long time, but not many had studied magnets in great detail. But people had noticed strange things. Benjamin Franklin ran electricity through needles and saw that they started behaving like magnets, attracting pieces of iron. Sailors reported that after their ship was struck by lightning, compass needles started pointing south instead of north. It was curious. When some scientists suggested that maybe electricity and magnetism are related in some way, most of them dismissed it as nonsense.

Danish physicist Hans Christian Oersted thought a little differently. He had been reading about *Naturphilosophie*, an approach to scientific study proposed by Friedrich Wilhelm Joseph Schelling. The idea of *Naturphilosophie* is that nature has to be understood as a whole and not as separate mathematical concepts. This was a slightly weird idea for that time, but it hinted that everything in nature is connected.

So Oersted tended to think that there was some relationship between magnetism and electricity. He designed experiments and demonstrated them during talks that he gave regularly to the public.

In one experiment, he set up a battery that produced electricity, connected wires to the battery and completed the circuit. Electric current flowed through the wire. Oersted wanted to put a compass needle near this set-up and see what would happen. For some reason, he wasn't able to try it out before the lecture, and so he tried it out during the lecture. To his great surprise, the compass needle shuddered and changed direction.

But this was such a small event that the audience wasn't impressed or simply did not notice. Oersted let it go.

Some sources suggest that this was a completely accidental discovery—that Oersted hadn't planned this experiment, but his notes suggest otherwise. Either way, the fact remains that he was aware enough to know that something was afoot!

After the lecture, he experimented in his lab. Once again, he connected the wires, completed the circuit and brought the compass needle near the wire. The compass needle moved. He changed the direction of the current in the wire, and the compass needle pointed in the opposite direction. He placed the compass at different points around the circuit, and each time, the needle moved the moment the current was switched on.

Oersted had just discovered that magnetism and electricity were related, and that electricity creates a magnetic field around it.

When he made his findings public, it led to a surge in studies. French scientist André-Marie Ampère discovered magnetic forces between wires that carried currents. Ten years later, Michael Faraday discovered that a magnetic field that is changing induces electricity in a conductor. Shortly after that, James Clerk Maxwell developed Maxwell's equations, which described how electricity and magnetism are related.

Electromagnetism became the basis of household appliances, industries, communication systems, medical systems—nearly everything that we now depend on in our everyday lives!

DID YOU KNOW?

You can make an electromagnet by looping a wire around a piece of iron (like a nail) and passing a current through the wire. The iron becomes a magnet as long as the current is flowing. An electromagnet is very useful—its magnetism can be turned on and off, unlike an ordinary magnet. Electromagnets are used in motors, generators, burglar alarms, electric bells, MRI machines and so on.

We've Discovered Nothing!

HOW ZERO AND THE DECIMAL SYSTEM CAME TO BE

Imagine you're in a math class in ancient Rome, and you've been asked to multiply 359 and 832. To start with, you would've had to write 359 as CCCLIX and 832 as DCCCXXXII. Then you would have had to add 359 to itself 832 times to get to the answer. Forget multiplication. Just imagine subtracting CCCLIX from DCCCXXXII. With absolutely no idea of zero, or the concepts of the units place and the tens place and so on, it would be enough to leave your brains all tangled up.

Mathematicians had to wrestle with their numbers until zero and the concept of numerical place came along. But how did it come about? Did zero just turn up one day? It was, in fact, a gradual evolution of ideas.

About 5000 years ago, ancient Mesopotamians used a character as a placeholder to denote nothingness. For example, if there was a row of numbers, and the last row had no entries in it, they just wrote two parallel lines instead of leaving it blank.

This was their way of saying that there was nothing in this row. But zero wasn't a number yet.

Some cultures didn't like the concept of nothingness—they thought it denoted chaos, or void, or emptiness. It made them uncomfortable, and they didn't even consider that it could be used for anything.

The concept of zero arose and flowered in India. We don't know when exactly this concept took shape. It must have been over centuries. But in the fifth century CE, Aryabhata wrote a mathematical work where he used nine digits, and a dot to denote zero. In the seventh century CE, Indian astronomer Brahmagupta wrote works in which he solved complex algebraic equations. Other scholars around the world had worked with these concepts too, but what Brahmagupta did was unique—he used zero in his calculations. Now, zero was no longer a placeholder, but an actual number. And if you could imagine a zero, you could imagine negative numbers too!

These three concepts had been floating around—the concept of zero, the concept of numerical place (units, tens, hundreds)

and the concept of the base 10 system (numbers 1 to 9, and zero). Indian mathematicians took these concepts and tied them up into a brilliantly simple system. With these ten digits, they could represent any number on earth, and calculations became ridiculously simple.

Arab travellers and merchants and knowledge-seekers took these ideas from India to the Arab world in the ninth and tenth centuries CE. Arabia itself was going through a period of immense growth in knowledge and culture. Muḥammad ibn-Mūsā al-Khwārizmī, a mathematician, used these Indian digits in his works.

In Pisa, Italy, Leonardo Fibonacci got his education from Arab mathematicians. It opened up a new world for him. He learnt these Indo-Arabic numerals, as they were now called. He wrote about them and used them in his work. More people came to know about it. It was a mind-blowing idea for those who grasped it.

But still, the western world rejected these numbers. They thought these ideas were against the church. They ignored and, in some cases, outlawed these ideas. Scholars and authorities may have rejected it, but merchants and traders knew what was good for them. They realized how practical this system was and used it in their day-to-day transactions. After that, there was no holding back. Today, the whole world uses them.

DID YOU KNOW?

The Sanskrit word for zero is shunya. It means emptiness. When Arabs translated that word into Arabic, it became sifr. In Latin, it got converted to zephirum. And from there comes the word zero.

Itty-bitty Teeny-Weeny Uncuttables

HOW WE CAME TO KNOW ABOUT THE ATOM

If someone gives you a wrapped present and asks you to guess what is in it without opening it, what would you do? Examine its shape and size. Weigh it in your hands to see if that gives you a clue. Shake it. Maybe hold it up to the light.

Now imagine trying to guess the structure of an object so tiny that you cannot even see it. That's what scientists faced when they wanted to find out about the atom. They had to figure out its structure just by testing how it behaved—and they got some unbelievable surprises.

The idea of the atom itself is very old. About 2500 years ago, Greek philosopher Democritus said that if you go on cutting an object into half, and half again and so on, there has to be a point where it cannot be cut any longer. He called this end particle atomos, which means 'uncuttable' in Greek, and said that all substances are made up of these particles. But his views weren't that popular because Aristotle, who was very influential, said that all matter is created out of fire, earth, water and air. Aristotle's views held for the next many centuries.

In the early 1800s, John Dalton proposed that matter is made up of indivisible atoms. A 100 years later, J.J. Thomson discovered that atoms have electrons in them.

But here was a little puzzle. An electron has a negative charge. But the atom is neutral. So, there must be something else in the atom that has a positive charge. The positive charge would then cancel out the electron's negative charge to keep the atom neutral.

Perhaps, said Thomson, the atom is like a plum pudding. The electrons (plums) are studded in a positive base (pudding), like chocolate chips in a cookie. This was called the 'plum pudding' model.

Is this really what an atom looked like? They were not sure yet.

cloud of +ve charge

-ve charge

If you cannot figure out what a gift is by its shape, size or weight, would you try throwing things at it? Well, Ernest Rutherford decided to check if the atom is like a plum pudding by throwing alpha particles at it. An alpha particle is a small positively charged particle. It is much heavier than an electron and moves fast. Rutherford took a very thin sheet of gold foil (1/3000 of an inch thick!) and decided to shoot alpha particles at it.

If the plum pudding model was correct, the heavy alpha particle should just shoot through the gold atoms and come out the other side, like a bullet going through a bag of sand.

Most of the alpha particles did behave like he thought they would. They passed straight through the gold foil. But here was the amazing part—some of the particles bounced right back.

Rutherford said, 'It was quite the most incredible event that has ever happened to me in my life. It was almost as incredible as if you fired a 15-inch shell at a piece of tissue paper and it came back and hit you.'

There was only one way to explain this result. There must be one small part in the atom that has a very concentrated positive charge. That part must contain almost all the mass of the atom. The alpha particles that bounced back were the ones that hit this small part, and were repelled because positive charge repels positive charge.

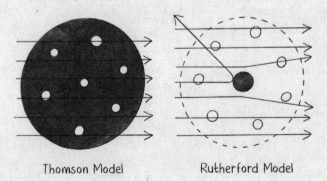

Thomson Model   Rutherford Model

Rutherford called this part nucleus (little nut in Latin). He also proposed that the electrons orbited this nucleus.

This model of the atom is accepted to this day, with some modifications. The atom is the smallest part of an element that still has the same properties of an element. At the centre of the atom is the nucleus, which has particles called protons and neutrons. Whizzing around the nucleus are the electrons. Protons are positively charged and electrons are negatively charged. Neutrons do not have a charge. The number of protons and electrons in an atom is the same.

DID YOU KNOW?

99.9 per cent of an atom is made up of empty space.

A proton is nearly 2000 times as heavy as an electron.

Niels Bohr suggested a modification that would explain why the electrons don't spin and get dragged into the nucleus. A few years later, Erwin Schrödinger proposed that electrons exist in what are called orbitals.

Click Click Click

One trillion. One followed by twelve zeroes. That's the number of photographs we humans took in 2019. That means that every second, there are 32,000 photos taken around the world. That's the kind of obsession we have about capturing images of ourselves and our world!

But it took a lot of imagination and hard work to get to this stage.

For millennia, humans have known how to project an image on a wall. All you need is a dark room, or a box, with a tiny hole on one of its walls. The outdoor scene can then be projected on the wall opposite the hole. This is the principle of the pinhole camera. It is also called the camera obscura (dark chamber in Latin). For centuries, people have used it for art, work, entertainment and to spy on unsuspecting passers-by.

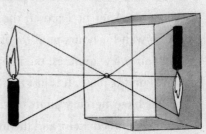

For a long time, we had no way to preserve that

145

image in the camera obscura. If you wanted a permanent image of yourself, you had to rely on an artist to paint you. That was expensive. So, most people went through life without a single likeness of themselves!

In the early 1800s, French inventor Joseph Nicéphore Niépce, who knew that silver salts became dark when exposed to daylight, coated a sheet with silver salts and placed it over the image in a camera obscura. The image imprinted itself on the sheet and he got a faint picture. But when he brought the sheet out of the dark room, bright daylight blackened the whole sheet. Frustrating. Niépce tried different chemicals and materials, until he hit upon a combination that worked.

He coated a metal plate with bitumen (a kind of petroleum product used for making roads). Bitumen hardens when exposed to light. He placed this metal plate in his camera obscura. On the plate, he projected the view from the first-floor window of his house. It took eight hours for an image to form on the plate. The bitumen that was exposed to light became hard. He washed the plate in lavender oil and turpentine. The unexposed bitumen, which remained soft, washed away. A permanent image was left behind!

Niépce started working with another Frenchman Louis Daguerre to make the process better. After Niépce died, Daguerre continued the work.

He used silver iodide on plates and arrived at an important realization. After he exposed the plate to the image, he didn't have to wait for hours until the image showed up on the plate. After only a few minutes, the image would have already started to form on the plate. It is just that he couldn't see the image yet. But if he blew mercury fumes on the exposed plates, he could see the image immediately, and the image stayed fixed.

He called this kind of image the daguerreotype.

Now if you wanted a photo of yourself, you would have to sit still for only a few minutes, not for eight hours.

At the same time, around 1840, Englishman William Henry Fox Talbot announced that he'd discovered a way to fix images too. Talbot washed sheets of paper with chemicals including silver nitrate and exposed them to the image. Then he washed the sheet with gallic acid to get a 'negative' of the image. After that, he could make a 'positive' by pressing another sheet treated with silver nitrate against this negative. Talbot called his technique calotype (calo—beautiful). This method had an advantage over the daguerreotype—they could make multiple copies of a single image.

English astronomer John Herschel, looking for a way to copy his notes, used hyposulphite of soda along with other chemicals,

and used a process similar to the calotype, to produce cyan (blue) and white images.

English botanist Anna Atkins used the cyanotype technique; pressed botanical specimens directly on to treated sheets and produced gorgeous images full of detail. She brought out the first book of photography ever. She is considered a pioneer in both botany and photography.

Once these techniques started becoming popular, more inventors tried to take better photographs and speed up the photo-taking process. Now you had to sit still for only a few seconds! Besides, until then, none of these techniques could make multiple copies of an image.

Cameras obscura gave way to bulky box cameras, which led to better, smaller, portable cameras. The 35 mm film followed— the adults around you will tell you that this was what they used in their childhood. Then, digital cameras arrived on the scene. Now, cameras have just slipped into smartphones, with tools and filters to get you the best pictures with the least effort.

DID YOU KNOW?

Cyanotype was also called blueprint. This method was used for making architectural and engineering drawings. That is why any kind of building plan, even if it is not blue, is called a blueprint!

The Bet That Launched the Movies

HOW MOVING PICTURES CAME ABOUT

How does a horse gallop? This was the question that occupied the mind of Leland Stanford in the late 1800s. Stanford had been the governor of California. He also built a portion of the transcontinental railroad in the US and had amassed wealth. He would also go on to start Stanford University. But at this point, he was a horse breeder. Automobiles weren't widespread, and horses were all-important.

Stanford wanted to know, in particular—when a horse gallops, is there any point at which all four of its feet are off the ground?

Yes, said Stanford. No, said some of his friends. Stanford took a bet with them to see who was right.

Stanford approached famous photographer Eadweard Muybridge. Could he take photographs of a running horse and solve this mystery for him?

Muybridge was famous for his landscape photographs. But photographing a moving object? Especially something as fast as a running horse? By the time Muybridge exposed the film to take one photograph, the horse would have finished galloping from one end of the field to another! How could he take photographs of each instant?

The key was to take photographs at many instants during the horse's run. If the film could not be exposed by hand, it would have to be done automatically somehow.

Muybridge got creative. He prepared a special racecourse between two walls. On one side of the track, he set up twelve cameras on a wall at waist height, at equal distances from one another. He painted the floors and the opposite wall white so that he would get a better contrast for his pictures. Next, he placed twelve wires across the racetrack, each wire connected to each of the twelve cameras. He hooked a cart, called a sulky, to the horse.

A driver drove the sulky on the racetrack. When the wheels of the sulky ran over a wire, the wire activated the camera to which it was attached. The camera automatically took a quick picture of the horse and the sulky. This way, he got twelve pictures of different instants during the horse's run.

Stanford and Muybridge conducted this experiment in front of an excited crowd. It was a resounding success. Twenty minutes after the horse ran, Muybridge developed the photographs and got twelve excellent pictures. He displayed them to the admiring onlookers. Stanford was proven right. All four legs of the horses were off the ground at one point! They could also see that when all four legs leave the ground, they gather near the middle of the horse's body, not outwards like in a rocking horse.

Muybridge later improved his techniques and took better photographs. He invented the zoopraxiscope. He traced each photograph on to different sections on a glass disc. When the

disc was spun fast, it created a moving picture of a galloping horse. (You can see this movie on YouTube—it looks like a gif!)

Remember, these photos were taken with different cameras. In 1882, the French physiologist Étienne-Jules Marey wanted to study movement, and became the first person to take a series of photographs with one camera, with successive images of a flying bird showing up on a single glass plate! In 1888, he replaced the glass plate with a long strip. It was the first 'film'—with 20 images per second—and was shown at the French Académie des Sciences!

Most of these inventions are such that the moment one person makes a breakthrough, a bunch of people use it as a springboard to experiment and innovate. Very soon, the motion picture camera came into being—and the world of entertainment changed forever!

DID YOU KNOW?

Movies are a series of photographs that we see one after the other very quickly. This works because of persistence of vision. When we look at an object, our eyes carry the image for a few seconds even after we turn away. Test it for yourself. Look at any object for a few seconds. Immediately, look at a plain wall or a plain piece of paper. You can see an image of that object on the wall or the piece of paper. When you look at a number of images that are slightly different, one after the other, they don't look like different images at all. They just look like continuous movement.

You can make your own movie. Take a little notepad and draw simple images on each page, with each image slightly different from the previous one. Flip the pages of the book, it will look like a movie!

All about Energy and the World's Most Famous Equation

E=MC²

In the 1700s, the idea of energy had been known for a while, and was defined as the ability of an object to do work. Kinetic energy is one form of energy. It is the energy that a body has due to its motion.

Sir Isaac Newton suggested that the kinetic energy of an object is E=mv, that is, it can simply be measured by multiplying the mass of the body and the velocity with which it moves. (Velocity is the speed of an object in a certain direction.)

So, said Newton, if an object that weighs 5 kg is moving at a speed of 10 km per hour, it has 50 (5 multiplied by 10) units of kinetic energy. But Newton didn't have any proof for this.

At the same time, a German mathematician Gottfried Leibniz said that, *nein*, it is not E=mv, but $E=mv^2$. But he had no proof either.

The British backed Newton and the Germans thought Leibniz was right.

Meanwhile, a remarkable pair in France turned their attention towards this matter.

Émilie du Châtelet was a clever young person. She had learned maths and physics and six languages. Her father was terrified that she wouldn't get married because she 'flaunts her mind' and drives away suitors. But he needn't have worried. She married a wealthy soldier and had three children. The writer Voltaire was her research companion.

Together with Voltaire, du Châtelet turned her husband's chateau into a research centre with a massive library and a well-equipped laboratory.

Du Châtelet was curious—mv or mv^2? She wanted experimental verification.

Meanwhile, a Dutch researcher Willem 's Gravesande was experimenting with dropping weights from various heights, on to a soft clay floor.

When an object is dropped on to a soft floor from a height, it sinks into the floor. How deep does it sink? That depends on

what the speed of the object was when it reached the floor. If E=mv is true, an object that has twice the speed should sink in two times deeper into the floor. But what he observed was that this object sank in *four* times deep. An object that had three times the speed, sank in *nine* times as deep.

This should only mean that kinetic energy depends on the square of the velocity. So Liebniz was right—it was mv^2. This was the kind of proof du Châtelet wanted. She did extensive calculus to back this up and published it in her books, along with other theories. Her books created waves in the scientific community and are still used by some to understand Newton's works!

We now know that the kinetic energy of a body is given by the formula $E = mv^2$. This formula makes it clear, that if v, the velocity of an object, is zero, E is also equal to zero. That is, when the body is not moving, it has no kinetic energy.

A couple of centuries later, Albert Einstein was calculating the kinetic energy of particles that move at very, very high speeds. These particles do not follow Newton's mechanics, the simple rules of motion that ordinary objects follow. So he used other formulae related to these high-speed particles for his calculations.

And then he found that there is a kind of energy that does not become zero even when the body is not moving. He called it rest energy. It is the amount of energy you would get if you converted the mass of the body into energy.

This is the equation:

$$E=mc^2$$

E is the energy that an object has. m is its mass.

c is the speed of light.

We know that light travels very fast. So, the speed of light is very, very large.

A large number multiplied by itself is a gargantuan number. So c^2 is enormous.

Going back to the equation, if you multiply the mass of an object with c^2, you get the energy of that object.

That means that every object contains a humongous, tremendous, whopping, monstrous, super-duper (you get the picture) amount of energy.

Wondering why you're feeling so tired and lazy if your body has so much energy? Remember, this is just the amount of energy that will be *available* if your body's mass is destroyed and converted into other forms of energy.

This equation changed a lot of things that scientists knew about the world. It is the most famous equation in the world and that is why people with absolutely no connection to science have heard of Einstein and his equation!

DID YOU KNOW?

$E=mc^2$ helped us understand the speed of light, and how the universe is expanding. It told us why the sun shines, helped figure out the structure of the atom and led to the creation of the atomic bomb (much to Einstein's sorrow). It also helps in space technology to generate power for telecommunication satellites.

Full Circle

Some things are so much a part of our lives that we don't even think of questioning them. Why are there 360 degrees in a circle? Why 360 longitude lines? Why 60 minutes in an hour? Why 60 seconds in a minute? What is this obsession with 60 and its multiples?

For the answer, we have to travel back in time.

We now use the base 10 system for all our calculations, based on the Indo-Arabic numerals. That is, we have 10 digits, 0 and 1 to 9. But 5000 years ago, the Babylonians used the base 60, or sexagesimal system, which they probably inherited from the Sumerians.

But why 60? We are not sure. One theory says that it was because two peoples, with different cultures, merged or interacted with each other. One set of people used the base 5 system: they based all their calculations on the number of fingers on one hand. But the other set used the base 12 system, because we have 12 segments in four fingers of one hand. Bend one of your fingers. There are three segments in it—three parts. So, using the thumb, if you count off the segments in each finger, you arrive at the number 12.

Now when these two groups traded, they used base 60, as it was something they could both understand and calculate with (5x12=60). The number 60 was convenient in many other ways. It has many divisors—1, 2, 3, 4, 5, 6, 10, 12, 15, 20, 30 and 60.

Now, let's come to 360.

Can you think of another number close to 360, which is an important number? That's right—365 days in a year.

Ancient people liked watching the stars. When we look at the night sky, some groups of stars appear to form patterns which we call constellations. These constellations move across the sky from

east to west during the night. At any time of the year, one of the constellations appears first on the eastern horizon as the sun sets. As the year progresses, another constellation takes the place of the first one, and then a third and so on. After a year, the first constellation appears again on the eastern horizon.

Each night, the constellation appeared at the eastern horizon at a position slightly different from the previous day—a small amount, a degree. So, in one year, the constellation moved 360 degrees, which completes a circle.

It is likely they knew that a year consists of more than 360 days, but 360 is a nice round number, and was probably enough for their purposes at that time. Besides, it also corresponded with the base 60 system—360 divided six times is 60!

Around 1500 BCE, Egyptians divided the day into 24 hours. But why 24? No one really knows why exactly, but the number 12 was important to them. After all, there were 12 lunar cycles in a year, and 12 major constellations—so that is probably why they divided the day into two 12-hour intervals: 10 daylight, 10 night hours, and two hours each of twilight.

Around the second century BCE, Greek astronomers divided the hours into small fractions. They used the base 60 system to divide it into 60 fractions—and that gave us minutes. A further 60 splits gave us seconds.

Even after the base 10 system came into being and became popular all over the world, these numbers stayed true to the Babylonian system. But look at this—when we want a second to be spilt into smaller bits, we use hundredths and thousandths! So, by the time a split second became important in our lives, we were already using the base 10 system, and that's what we went with.

DID YOU KNOW?

An equilateral triangle is one in which all three sides are of equal length. The angles are all 60 degrees each. A circle can hold six equilateral triangles—the length of the side of each triangle is the same as the radius of the circle. And 6 times 60 degrees is 360 degrees.

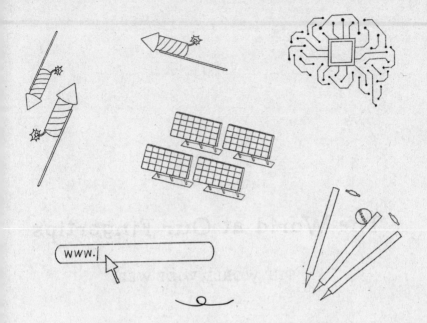

MODERN LIFE AND
LATEST DISCOVERIES

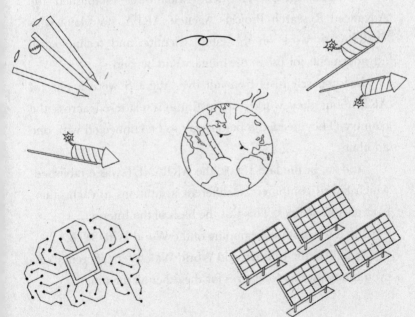

The World at Our Fingertips

THE WORLD WIDE WEB

After World War II, the US and the Soviet Union were locked in a cold war marked by fear and rivalry. In 1957, it came to a head—the Soviet Union launched Sputnik 1, the first artificial satellite, beating the US in the race to space.

In response, US President Eisenhower established the Advanced Research Projects Agency (ARPA, now known as DARPA) to work on the latest scientific and technological advancements for use in the military and beyond.

Leading scientists from all over the US were a part of ARPA, but they worked at institutions scattered across the country. They needed a better way to be connected with one another.

And so, in the late 1960s, the ARPANET was established, which linked computers at different institutions to each other, over telephone lines. This was the basis of the Internet.

But it was not the beginning of the World Wide Web.

Wait. Are the Internet and World Wide Web different? Yes, even though we use one term for the other all the time.

The Internet is a global network of computers, usually connected over telephone lines. The World Wide Web is an application that runs on the Internet. When you Google for information, you are using the Web *over* the Internet. The Web is a collection of websites, images, videos and photos that you access *over* the Internet.

How did the Web come about? After ARPANET, local computer. networks became pretty common, especially for official and research uses.

Then, CERN, the European Organization for Nuclear Research in Geneva, Switzerland, faced a problem. The world's best scientists visited CERN for research. But they found it hard to collaborate with each other as they all used different kinds of computers, programming language and applications. Though files and information could be shared between computers (like file transfers, using FTP—file transfer protocol), it was different for each kind of computer and program.

They needed an easy-to-use system common to all computers and systems to make information sharing seamless. Tim Berners-Lee, a young software engineer, thought of a way to solve this problem. In 1989, he developed the World Wide Web. It made use of a new technology called hypertext.

The World Wide Web had three main features, which we still use today. It would use HTML, or Hypertext Markup Language, a common formatting language for the Web, that everybody could use.

An identifier, a unique link or address, would identify each resource on the Web—we now call this the URL.

And http—Hypertext Transfer Protocol—would be a way for users on a web browser to have a 'conversation' with a web server, and get the information they need.

The Web at CERN was a success. Then, Berners-Lee realized that for the Web to be truly useful, it should not be owned or controlled by anybody. Everyone must be able to use it without having to pay for it, or ask for permission. So, he made the code freely available to everybody, forever. This was remarkable, in a world where every little discovery or technique is patented, and information jealously guarded!

Thanks to this, in the 1990s, the world exploded with creativity, imagination, collaboration and innovation. The world has never been the same again!

DID YOU KNOW?

The first webpage that Tim Berners-Lee put up still exists! Check it out here: http://info.cern.ch/ hypertext/WWW/TheProject.html

Follow the Water!

We're curious about our neighbours—peering at them, wondering what they are like . . . Wait, did you think I was talking about next-door neighbours? Naughty, naughty! I meant our neighbours in space! We've been spying on the moon, the planets and the stars for a long time. But we're most interested in Mars, and for good reason. Mars is a lot like Earth. Similar in size, it is in the Goldilocks zone (not too hot, not too cold). Could it mean that Mars has life too, like Earth does?

The first step to finding that out is to see if there is water on Mars. But why is the search for water so important? The presence of liquid water might help scientists find life, or the building blocks of life—that is, how life came into existence on Earth. This is why many space programs work according to the mantra 'Follow the water'. Orbiters, landers and rovers designed to search for life have all gone looking for water, because that is where life, if any, would be found.

In the nineteenth century, Italian astronomer Giovanni Schiaparelli observed hazy streaks on Mars, and called them

'canali', the Italian word for channels. But it was translated into English as canals, giving the impression that these were not made by natural processes, but built—by aliens? This made Percival Lowell, an American astronomer, map out an entire network of Mars canals. These ideas in turn influenced author H.G. Wells, who wrote *The War of the Worlds*, which ultimately gave birth to speculation about Martians and little green men. But, in reality, there are no Martian-made canals out there—it is human tendency to want to find patterns in everything.

In 1971, *Mariner 9* was sent to orbit Mars, becoming the first spacecraft to orbit another planet. It sent back photographs of what looked like dry riverbeds and canyons. Did that mean water did exist on Mars in the past? Four years later, Viking spacecrafts landed on Mars, and sent back data that pointed to water under the surface of Mars. But the data was not conclusive.

In the 1990s, a number of Mars missions gave us a great deal of information. Some found minerals, which indicated the presence of water. Other data suggested there was ice under the surface of Mars.

In 2000, NASA's Mars Global Surveyor spacecraft found formations like gullies—ravines formed by flowing water—yet again suggesting that perhaps water had flowed there in the past. Recent studies suggest that these ravines were probably formed by flowing sand, not water.

In the early 2000s, the two Mars Exploration Rovers (MER) Spirit and Opportunity found traces of water inside rocks. And then Spirit broke one of its wheels. But this stumble turned out to be fortunate! The broken wheel scraped into the surface of Mars, and reached a layer rich in silica, which was most likely formed in the presence of water.

Meanwhile, the Phoenix Mars Lander reached Mars in 2008 to study Martian soil. It turned up small chunks of material that disappeared after a few days, making scientists think that they must be pieces of water ice. Phoenix then detected water vapour in a sample that it collected. More excitement! But is there any liquid water at all?

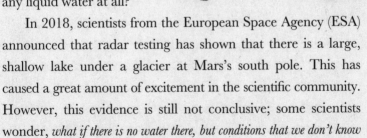

In 2018, scientists from the European Space Agency (ESA) announced that radar testing has shown that there is a large, shallow lake under a glacier at Mars's south pole. This has caused a great amount of excitement in the scientific community. However, this evidence is still not conclusive; some scientists wonder, *what if there is no water there, but conditions that we don't know of yet just make it appear as though there is water?*

So, you see how particular scientists are about strong evidence! They're all tuned in to see what we'll find next.

Will we find more information that will tell us the history of Mars and why it is a wasteland? And most importantly—will it be possible for human beings to live on Mars sometime in the future?

DID YOU KNOW?

SpaceX, a company founded by Elon Musk (of Tesla fame), has been working on Mars missions, and has recently unveiled the first version of a spaceship to Mars, called Starship. They aim to send humans to Mars as early as within the next decade. Scientists are studying how humans can live on Mars, the kind of buildings they would need, the energy sources, the food they would need to grow and other nitty-gritties.

Car, Drive Thyself

SELF-DRIVING VEHICLES

One day in a Californian desert in 2004, thousands of people gathered for a car race. But this wasn't just any car race; these cars had no drivers.

The race was the idea of DARPA, the research department of the US Defence Agency. The primary cause of soldier deaths during wars is military vehicles being targeted or bombed. So, DARPA was looking to develop driverless cars (also called self-driving cars), and had spent millions in research already. But they hadn't progressed much.

They invited driverless cars from around the world to complete a 142-mile track. The award was a million dollars.

The teams arrived. The race began. In no time, it was apparent that the race was going to be a disaster. One vehicle turned turtle. Another crashed into a wall. Yet another got tangled with a wire fence. One car developed at Carnegie Mellon University showed some promise at first. It drove for 7 miles, until it hit a hill and stalled. Its wheels started turning in place, until the vehicle caught fire. And that was that.

The organizers had to jump into a helicopter, fly to the finish line and tell the waiting journalists to go home.

However, DARPA had better luck at the race the following year. This time, five cars completed the race successfully, and driverless cars were well on their way.

The idea of driverless cars isn't new. Back in the fifteenth century, Leonardo da Vinci had designed a cart with a wound-up spring that propelled the cart forward.

The first efforts to actually build a driverless car started about a 100 years ago. The Houdina Radio Control Company guided a car through the traffic of New York using radio signals sent by another car that followed close behind it. Of course, this was just a demonstration of the possibilities. There's no point in a driverless car if you need another car with a driver to tail it all the time!

At the 1939 New York World's Fair, Norman Bel Geddes, an industrialist, introduced 'Futurama'. It was a vision of the future of the world, with an automated highway on which cars drove themselves. A team led by General Motors introduced a stretch of highway in the US in the 1950s, based on Geddes's ideas. Electronic circuits were built into the road. The cars had sensors that could pick up signals from the road, and could be told how and where to drive.

The UK also began research into these driverless car road systems, but they all ran out of funding. It was turning out to be too expensive.

That was when engineers realized they had to stop trying to make the roads smarter, and try to make the cars themselves smarter.

In 1977, Japanese researchers came up with what many consider the first truly self-driving vehicle. This car had two built-in cameras. A computer analysed the surrounding areas using the images from these cameras. Then, it instructed the car on how to drive. However, this car crawled forward at only 20 miles an hour.

A German aerospace engineer called Ernst Dickmanns fitted a Mercedes van with sensors and cameras that collected data, and sent it to a computer which told the van what to do with the steering wheel and brake. The system concentrated on filtering out unnecessary data and zeroing in on only the relevant data. In 1987, this vehicle, called VaMoRs, drove on Germany's Autobahn at an impressive 60 miles an hour!

Research continued all over the world, but as can be seen in the 2004 flop car race, the technology was still not quite there yet.

In 2010, Google entered the scene. They started by hiring engineers who had worked on the DARPA cars, and proceeded with research. Google's cars have now driven millions of miles, mostly without accident. Uber, Microsoft, Tesla, as well as traditional car manufacturers are all now working on self-driving cars. After all, it appears to be the future!

DID YOU KNOW?

It is very difficult to program self-driving cars with all the situations that come up during driving. For example, if you are driving on a narrow road and there's an ambulance behind you, you would probably drive up the footpath and let the ambulance pass. Now how do you tell a self-driving car that this is okay in only some situations? There are questions of ethics too. If a car has only two choices in an emergency—apply brakes to avoid hitting the deer crossing the road, or swerve at the risk of hitting or being hit by a vehicle—what is the right thing to do? How do you teach a car something that you know might not be right in every situation? So, the challenges go beyond technology!

The Source of Life

Ever used a magnifying glass to focus the rays of the sun and burn paper? You'll like this story.

In 212 BCE, the Romans laid siege to Syracuse. Marcellus, the Roman general, docked his ships a little away from land, just out of reach of the arrows of the warriors of Syracuse. What should Syracuse do? Just sit back and wait for the enemy to attack? That was when Archimedes stepped up with a beautifully nerdy solution. He arranged a number of small mirrors such that at midday they reflected the sun's rays and focused them on a single point—the enemy ship. The ships caught fire and burnt to ashes.

Is this a true story? We don't know. But is it possible to actually do this? We don't know about then, but today, yes!

Humans have been using solar energy for a long while now. Well, technically, we've been using solar energy ever since we were single-celled organisms. But when did we consciously start making the heat and light of the sun work for us in other ways? Now that is a more valid question.

The answer: Perhaps about 9000 years ago, when humans used naturally occurring glass to concentrate the rays of the sun—to start a fire, of course!

In the following centuries, humans built structures that used the sun's rays to heat buildings naturally.

When the heat energy of the sun is put to human use, it is referred to as solar thermal energy. Apart from heating and cooking, the heat from the sun is used to produce electricity too!

Solar thermal electricity generators use the same principle as in Archimedes's story. Large mirrors in the shape of a parabola (an open curve, somewhat like a cup, but flatter) concentrate sunlight on to a tube that contains a liquid. The heated liquid passes through a heat exchanger, where it heats up water. This water turns into steam. The steam then turns a turbine, just like liquid water turns a turbine in a hydroelectric plant. The turbine runs a generator; electricity is produced.

In November 2019, Heliogen, a clean energy company, announced a major breakthrough. It discovered a way to use artificial intelligence and an entire field of mirrors to reflect so much sunlight that it generates very high temperatures—up to 1000 degree Celsius! This is nearly a quarter of the surface temperature of the sun! This would help industries like cement and steel that require extremely high temperatures. This technology has the potential to replace fossil fuels and reduce CO_2 emissions.

We can also produce energy directly from sunlight. This is called photovoltaic energy and has become increasingly popular in the last 200 years. Photovoltaic (PV) or solar cells make use of the photoelectric effect—when light falls on certain surfaces, it releases electrons which can be made to flow as electric current.

One of the first uses of photovoltaic energy was in space technology. It is difficult and heavy to carry power-generating devices to space. So why not create your own energy right there in space using solar panels installed on the spacecraft? It's like taking a cooker with you on your travels to cook food, rather than pack and carry lots of food.

Today, entire homes and buildings are powered by solar technology. Researchers are trying to make solar technology more efficient and less expensive, so that its use can become widespread.

DID YOU KNOW?

In 2019, Bertrand Piccard completed the first zero-emissions flight around the world with Solar Impulse 2, the world's largest and most powerful solar-powered airplane.

Up, Up and Away

ROCKETS

The magnificent, awe-inspiring rockets that zoom into space today are a result of two thousand years of inspiration, brilliance, hard work—and some spectacular flop shows.

In the sixteenth century, Wan Hu, a Chinese stargazer, dreamed of flying into space. He built a chair and attached forty-seven gunpowder rockets to its base. He sat on it and got assistants to run up to his chair and fire up all the rockets at the same time. They did so, ran back and waited. There was a huge explosion. When the smoke cleared up, Wan Hu was nowhere to be seen. Some believed that he actually made it to the moon, and that he is, in fact, the man on the moon!

Rockets are based on Newton's Third Law of Motion—every action has an equal and opposite reaction. Blow air into a balloon. Now let go of the end. The air rushes out of the mouth. At the same time, the balloon experiences an equal force in the opposite direction. This is how rockets and jet planes work too.

The first such device recorded is from the fourth century BCE. Archytas, a Greek mathematician, created a wooden dove

and made it fly up to 200 m, powered by a jet of steam or compressed air.

The earliest rockets probably started off as fireworks. The thirteenth-century Chinese packed tubes of bamboo with gunpowder. When one end was ignited, the thrust of the gases escaping propelled the tube forward. They also attached these rockets to arrows and used them against the invading Mongol armies.

Rockets continued to be used in warfare in the following centuries. Like all technology necessary for warfare, a lot of attention and money was spent on improving rockets. Kazimierz Siemienowicz, a Polish-Lithuanian commander in the Polish Royal Artillery, was an expert in rocketry. In the early 1600s, he wrote detailed designs of rockets for use in both fireworks and warfare. Some of his designs and ideas are a part of the basic rocket technology of today.

In the late 1700s, Tipu Sultan of Mysore used rockets to astonishing results in his wars against the British. His rockets used high-quality iron tubes, instead of the weak wooden tubes that were previously used. Iron tubes could hold more gunpowder, and the rockets went higher, faster and farther. The British armies were left completely stunned. Later on, William Congreve, a British colonel, studied Tipu's rocket technology and made his own improvements. He also developed ways to launch rockets from ships.

In the 1900s, American college professor and scientist Robert Goddard built the first rocket fuelled by liquid propellants (fuel that is used to propel rockets). It didn't fly too high, just the height of a four-storey building, but it was a good beginning!

With World War II, rockets were built as weapons of mass destruction. Germany was a hotbed of rocket studies. Hermann Oberth made great strides in rocketry and was responsible for the deadly V-2 rockets with which the Nazis pummelled London in World War II.

After the war, all eyes turned towards space. Several German rocket scientists emigrated to the Soviet Union and the United States, and assisted them in the Space Race, as the two countries tripped over each other to demonstrate technological and military superiority. The result? Extremely fast improvements in rockets and space technology!

The Soviet Union launched *Sputnik 1*, an artificial satellite, in 1957. Laika the dog became the first living creature to go to space, and Yuri Gagarin, the first human.

In 1969, the US sent humans to the moon and brought them back safely.

Since then, increasingly advanced spacecrafts have been launched from rockets. They've gone deep into space—and have sent back stunning pictures of our solar system. The *Voyager 1* spacecraft was even able to leave the solar system and go to interstellar space.

Many countries have built and sent rockets up with satellites for communication, weather, military and other purposes. India is one of the forerunners in space technology, and India's Mangalyaan, the Mars Orbiter Mission, has been a grand success.

Experts predict that rockets in the future will be able to carry larger satellites, and even multiple satellites at the same time. Research is also ongoing to find safer, more efficient rocket fuels, which are also better for the environment.

DID YOU KNOW?

Escape velocity is a measure of how fast a rocket has to travel to escape the gravitational pull of the planet. For Earth, it is 11 km per second! At that speed, you can cover the width of India in less than five minutes!

Can Machines Really Take Over the World?

ARTIFICIAL INTELLIGENCE

Machines that think for themselves. Machines that can make decisions. It used to be the stuff of science fiction. Not anymore.

Siri or Alexa answering your questions. Netflix suggesting new shows based on what you have already watched. Gmail completing your sentences. Google's search suggestions. Amazon suggesting new products to your parents, based on what they have bought. Machines can now even make calls and fool the listener into thinking it is a real human calling.

All these are possible because of the development of artificial intelligence (AI). AI is the science and engineering of making intelligent machines. AI has made it possible for machines to process large amounts of data—words, numbers, pictures and so on—and recognize patterns. Based on the pattern it sees, it can make decisions. It is almost as if it can learn from experience and perform tasks that are human-like. This is called machine learning.

The road to where we are now in terms of AI has been exciting, but rocky.

One of the first people to come up with an idea of an intelligent machine was Alan Turing, an English mathematician and code-breaker. Humans use logic, and the information available to them, to solve problems and make decisions. So, asked Turing, can't we teach machines to do the same thing?

In 1950, Turing proposed a test for machines, now known as the Turing test. A machine is said to pass the Turing test if a human talks to a computer and is unable to tell if she is talking to a machine or a human.

What stopped Turing from working on machine learning right then? Well, he was ready, but computers weren't. The computers of 1950 couldn't store commands. They could do what they were told to do, but couldn't be made to remember what they did. Besides, computers were super expensive.

In 1956, American computer scientist John McCarthy organized a conference in the US, where, for the first time, people got together to talk about the possibilities of machine learning. McCarthy used the term 'artificial intelligence' for the first time at this conference. Along with American scientist Marvin Minsky, he set up an AI lab at MIT. The US government funded the research, hoping that AI would help them in the Cold War against the Soviet Union. But years passed, and the researchers didn't have much to show for their efforts; computers were still not ready.

For about two decades, there was a lull, a period known as the 'AI Winter', before research picked up again. Computers got better, and money for research started pouring in again.

One technique that helped advance AI technology was to focus on a specific area—like chess. If we teach a machine a lot of

chess moves, will it be able to defeat a human? Scientists worked on it, and in 1997, Deep Blue, a supercomputer, defeated chess grandmaster Garry Kasparov. Kasparov was surprised at how human Deep Blue seemed to be—some of its decisions seemed to him like they were based on human-like intuition. He even argued that there must have been a human behind the controls.

AI in the twenty-first century is progressing in leaps and bounds. Sixty years to the day that Alan Turing passed away, a chatbot (a computer program designed to chat with humans) was created and named Eugene Goostman (with the personality of a thirteen-year-old Ukrainian boy who owned a pet hamster). Goostman convinced one out of three judges that it was human. But many think that Eugene Goostman was 'taught' how to cheat the judges, and don't consider that it truly passed the test.

Eugene Goostman
THE WEIRDEST CREATURE IN THE WORLD

Type your question here

I

reply

So, the research continues!

DID YOU KNOW?

In 1950, Isaac Asimov wrote a collection of stories
called *I, Robot*. He imagined the future of machine
intelligence. Science fiction stories like these help
scientists imagine futuristic scenarios. It helps us
think ahead. It inspires us to ask—what if? Many
times, it is through these stories that scientists
can imagine what can be done, and work towards
that future.

Aaaaaand . . . It's OUT!

CRICKET UMPIRING

14 November 1992. India's tour of South Africa. It is the first Test of the series, and India is batting. India has lost two wickets early and is on shaky ground. Nineteen-year-old Sachin Tendulkar joins Ravi Shastri at the crease. They hold for a while and put on a few runs. And then the historic moment arrives. Tendulkar is on 11. Brian McMillan bowls a delivery. Tendulkar hits the ball and tries to take a single. The ball coasts to expert fielder Jonty Rhodes, who catches it and sends it flying towards the stumps. Tendulkar quickly tries to get back to the crease. Andrew Hudson catches Rhodes's throw and breaks the stumps. The crowd roars. Is Tendulkar in? Is he out? It's too close for the umpire to figure out!

For the first time in cricketing history, the third umpire is consulted. Karl Liebenberg, the third umpire, watches the replay. It is clear to him. Sachin is out! The green light goes on (green was out and red was not out, at that time). Sachin walks back to the pavilion, the first cricketer to be declared out by a third umpire!

An umpire or referee in any game needs to be trained and knowledgeable about the nitty-gritties of the game. They should be calm, alert, unbiased, fair, level-headed and completely professional. Being an umpire is a position of immense pressure and great responsibility.

But an umpire is human. And humans make mistakes. Even a tiny error can change the course of a game; it can arouse the anger of passionate players and fans and snowball into a disaster!

That is why it's nice if an umpire can get a little help from technology!

It's hard to imagine how any sport was judged before the advent of technology. Imagine a 100-m sprint with runners crossing the finish line neck to neck. Now, we have replays that play the race in extreme slow motion to determine the winner to a thousandth of a second. But previously, they had to rely on guesswork, and mistakes were all too common.

It is the same in cricket. Some umpiring decisions are easy to make, but others are tricky—especially leg before wicket, or LBW, where the ball would have struck the wicket if it had not been obstructed by the batsman's leg.

With the advent of television and video recording, action replays and slow-motion technology removed the uncertainty in close run-outs like in Tendulkar's case. The third umpire proved invaluable—it was good to have another pair of eyes to pause, slow down and zoom into the action and give clear and fair decisions.

SpiderCam is a camera high above the stadium, connected by cables, able to travel around the stadium and give a 360-degree view of the entire action. Snickometer is a technology in which a tiny microphone on one of the stumps records sounds and analyses it. The sound pattern determines whether the ball made

contact with the bat, or whether it hit the batsman's body or pads, or the ground.

Some technologies started off as military technology and were then adapted to cricket.

The military often makes use of thermal imaging technology, in which infrared cameras sense heat, not light. The higher the temperature, the more infrared radiation an object releases, and so the image captured by infrared sensors are brighter. Thermal imaging technology is used to find the location of enemy tanks, fighter jets and even people (we emit radiation too). This is useful especially when it is dark or there is smoke and dust, and visibility is not very good.

This is the technology used in Hot Spot, in cricket, to determine where the ball has made contact with the bat or the body. Two thermal-imaging cameras placed on the field capture the heat that is generated when one object hits another. This shows up as a bright white spot, a hot spot. It is invaluable in LBW decisions.

Hawk-eye tracks the trajectory of a moving ball. It is used in missile technology to calculate the potential paths of missiles. Paul Hawkins, a cricketing enthusiast with a PhD in artificial intelligence, came up with the idea of using it for sport. A series of cameras are placed around the field. They capture images of the ball from different angles and determine the path of the ball. Hawk-eye tracks the ball, and estimates its projected path—it is great for LBW decisions. Hawk-eye technology is used in other sports too, like tennis.

But not everybody is a fan of these technologies, mainly because they slow down the game. Earlier the umpire on the field would take a decision and the game would go on. But now we have to wait until the third umpire gets back before the game can proceed. But as technology progresses, we can hope that decisions will become faster and fairer.

DID YOU KNOW?

It could be possible to use image processing technology and automate decisions for run-outs and stumping. A computer analyses thousands of images of run-outs and 'learns' to determine when it is a run-out and when it is not. With more technology, and with advancements in artificial intelligence, do you think we will reach a point where human umpires on the field would not be necessary at all?

Check It Out!

A barcode is the pattern of parallel lines of different widths that you see on the price tag of your new clothes, or on the packaging of an item in the supermarket. The cashier scans the barcode and tells you how much you need to pay. But why do we need barcodes, anyway? Can't the cashier just read the price on all the items, add it up (mentally, using pencil and paper or with a calculator or computer) and then tell you how much it cost?

As long as it is a small store with just a few items, such methods work just fine. In fact, these were the common methods before barcodes came into the picture.

Then, stores became larger and started stocking thousands of items. How do you keep track of all the items in the store and what items are running out? If there is a discount on a particular item, will the cashier be able to remember to apply the discount each time that item turns up? Besides, when people buy a large number of items, checking out takes a long, long time. It is laborious and things can easily go wrong—items missed out, or counted twice, mistakes in addition, not to mention the long lines of people waiting for their turn to checkout.

People started thinking of ways to automate the whole checkout process. In the 1930s, some people toyed with the idea of an automated grocery store, involving punch cards. These were stiff bits of paper with holes punched into them according to a code, and held information. In some places, punch cards were used for voting in elections, and came in handy to input data into the earliest computers. What if shoppers could punch holes into cards, denoting what they needed? The cashier could then load them into a reader/scanner, which would trigger a process where the required items from the racks would arrive on a moving carousel, and a bill would be generated automatically.

It was a good idea, but too expensive to put together, especially when the world was going through the Great Depression.

In 1950, the head of a local supermarket chain in Philadelphia got frustrated at the delays at the checkout counters. He asked the dean of Drexel Institute of Technology if there was a solution available that would get shoppers to move through the checkout line more quickly. If it could help him check stocks in his warehouse, even better. A student, Bob Silver, overheard the conversation and mentioned it to his friend Joe Woodland.

Woodland went to his grandparents' house on the beach, turning ideas over in his head. As he was lounging on the sand, he idly drew dots and dashes of the Morse code in the sand. He put his fingers on the marks and drew the fingers towards himself, forming narrow and wide lines in the sand. Inspiration struck. A combination of thick and thin lines that carry information about each item would work well!

But how would a human look at and understand the information a barcode holds? Woodland then built a scanner that

would 'read' the lines and convert it into numbers. Woodland and Silver modified the design further, with thick and thin lines in concentric circles, and got a patent for it.

However, scanning technology was still in its infancy and so barcodes did not take off. Over the next two decades, large manufacturers made their own codes for their products, while supermarket owners printed their own versions on the products. It was too confusing. What was needed was a system the entire world could use.

In the 1970s, Alan Haberman, vice president of a chain of grocery stores in Boston, formed a committee to choose a universal standard system. They zeroed in on a design created by George Laurer of IBM. This is the modern barcode.

In 1974, in a historic moment, a supermarket cashier in Ohio scanned the first barcode on a pack of Wrigley's chewing gum!

As barcodes become more advanced, they hold more information than ever before: details about the product, price, manufacturing date, how it was shipped, who checked the product and so on.

Barcodes are now used in other fields too: by airlines to tag boarding passes and luggage, in hospitals to tag newborn babies, and to keep track of anything starting from animals and rental cars to nuclear waste. They even help beekeepers monitor the movement of honeybees through teeny-tiny barcodes or QR codes on the backs of bees!

DID YOU KNOW?

Different versions of the barcode have made life even easier: you can pull up a website using a QR code, and even pay for products.

Barcodes are becoming even smaller, thanks to advances in nanotechnology. The bokode, developed in MIT, is a tiny data tag that holds much more information than an ordinary barcode or QR code. It can be read by an ordinary smartphone camera from great distances!

Creating Your Own Things

3D PRINTING

Take a piece of paper, draw a square on it and colour it in with a thick layer of paint. Once it dries, apply another thick layer of paint on it. If you go on applying layers of paint on it, the paint starts to stand out of the surface. Go on for long enough and you should end up with a cube!

That is how a 3D printer works.

A regular 2D printer applies ink on to paper and prints out a sheet of paper. The 3D printer adds a third dimension—height. There is no paper, just the base on which the layers are built up. The 'ink' in this case is the material, like plastic, which is laid over each previous layer to make up the object.

Just like you send a document or an image file to the 2D printer, you send instructions to a 3D printer as well—just that the file is much more detailed. A computer makes a mathematical model of the object you need to print, and slices the model into a large number of thin layers. Information about each layer is contained in a different file. All these files are packaged into one big file and sent to the 3D printer.

This sounds like the latest technology, doesn't it? Actually, 3D printing is nearly forty years old!

In the 1980s, a Japanese researcher, Hideo Kodama, and a team of French engineers, working separately, discovered different ways to print layers of material to create an object. But Kodama could not file for a patent in time, due to funding issues, and the work of the French engineers did not take off, again because of a lack of funding. So, the credit for discovering 3D printing usually goes to Charles Hull.

Charles Hull worked in a company that used ultraviolet light to make coatings for furniture. At that time, if industrial designers wanted to try out new designs for which they needed specific parts, they had to wait for weeks and months until those parts were manufactured and delivered to them. They were looking for ways to create these parts themselves and speed up the process of innovation.

Hull wondered if he could use UV technology to place thousands of layers of material, one on top of the other, and create three-dimensional objects. He worked in his lab for months and discovered a method of 3D printing using what is referred to as stereolithography (stereo—3D effect; lithography—a process of printing).

Hull worked with a photopolymer, a material that changes from liquid to solid when light shines on it. A computer used a beam of UV light to draw each layer of the object being built, on the surface of a vat full of the photopolymer. The layer turned solid and was removed. He set it up so that each hardened layer was removed and piled up one on top of the previous one—and built up a 3D object.

Hull started a 3D printing company. At that time, he himself wasn't aware of all that this technology was capable of, that is,

until 1996, when 3D printing was used for a medical procedure. Surgeons were trying to separate conjoined twins who shared a leg bone. The doctors thought that only one of the twins would be able to walk after they were separated. Then, they took scans of the leg bone and created a 3D model of it. The model made it clear that the bone was large enough to be split, and both twins would be able to walk! The surgery was successful.

3D printing has also been used in food, cars, musical instruments, jewellery, clothes, shoes, furniture, toys and art and in the automobile and aeroplane industry. Archaeologists and palaeontologists can recreate old artefacts and fossils using this technology. Physicians and dentists can make hearing aids, prosthetics and artificial teeth. They replicate models of organs and tumours to study them, and to plan complicated surgeries in advance using 3D models of organs and the human body.

But 3D printing could be put to dangerous and illegal use too. A man in the US printed a gun and fired a shot from it. Since such guns are made of plastic, they can cheat metal detectors.

They do not have any identification numbers like regular guns do and cannot be traced back to the owner. It could allow criminals to go undetected. However, fortunately, 3D printing a gun is not as easy as it sounds!

DID YOU KNOW?

You can even print a 3D printer! Well, almost. You can print most of the individual parts of a 3D printer and then assemble them all together. The next step in medical science is to actually print an organ on a 3D printer. Is it possible at all? Perhaps in the future!

Scientists have 3D printed the voice box of the mummy of Nesyamun, who lived during the reign of Ramses XI, and they've produced sound from it. Now they know what Nesyamun sounded like!

Warning about Warming

They worked long hours in pursuit of evidence. They endured physical and mental hardship, travelling to remote places in search of data. They made what sounded like outlandish statements, putting their reputations at stake. They struggled for funding, because nobody believed them. But finally—and much too late—the world sat up and listened to what these scientists had been saying for a long time, that over the last 150 years or so, the earth's climate has changed due to human activity, and it has led to disastrous consequences for the world.

Humans have long suspected that some human activities have an effect on nature. For instance, cutting down trees leads to less rainfall. But mostly, it was thought that humans were too tiny and unimportant to affect the forces of mighty Mother Nature.

In the 1800s, French scientist Joseph Fourier described the earth's greenhouse effect: that the atmosphere of the earth traps the heat of the sun and warms the earth, and does not allow this heat to escape. Irish physicist John Tyndall concluded from his experiments that this greenhouse effect is caused by the presence of water vapour and various gases in the atmosphere that absorb the heat. The more greenhouse gases there are, the warmer the earth becomes.

In the late 1800s, Swedish chemist Svante Arrhenius declared that human activity is causing an increase in the earth's greenhouse effect. He said that ever since the Industrial Revolution, humans have been burning tonnes of coal and releasing a gargantuan amount of carbon dioxide into the atmosphere. Carbon dioxide is the most important greenhouse gas, and as a result, the earth is getting warmer. But many scientists did not believe him.

Evidence. That's what scientists need. In search of crucial numbers, in the 1930s, British engineer G.S. Callendar studied data from 147 weather stations around the world, recorded over many decades. It was clear that temperatures around the world had been constantly rising.

And yet, he was met with disbelief.

Perhaps the world would take notice if you showed them that the levels of carbon dioxide have increased. Scientist C.D. Keeling developed an accurate technique of measuring carbon dioxide in the air. He set up observatories at Antarctica and Hawaii, and painstakingly monitored and measured the level of carbon dioxide in the air. As the months passed, a pattern emerged, of natural and man-made variations in the levels of carbon dioxide. His measurements showed that with each year, the carbon dioxide in the atmosphere increased.

In the next couple of decades, international organizations were set up to study and monitor the climate. Better technology led to more accurate measurements, and the advent of computers made it easy to study data. Scientists could predict future trends more accurately.

Evidence of climate change started accumulating. The world initially reacted with curiosity, which quickly changed to concern, then anxiety and now—full-blown panic.

Governments and organizations have introduced rules and protocols to reduce carbon emissions. But we are nowhere near controlling or managing the crisis. This is made worse by the fact that many people in power refuse to accept the evidence that climate change is real.

The effects of climate change, though, are quite obvious. The oceans have become warmer. Ice sheets and glaciers are melting, causing sea levels to rise and threatening to flood coastal areas. Due to changes in temperature, there are changes to patterns in wind, rainfall and ocean currents. This leads to an increase in floods, hurricanes, wildfires, bush fires and other natural disasters.

All these changes affect plant and animal life, and consequently, human life too.

It is time to stop talking and start acting on climate change.

DID YOU KNOW?

How do we know how much carbon dioxide there was in the past centuries? One way to find out is by drilling ice cores. Imagine a glass full of layers of crushed ice, of different colours. Now put a straw into the glass, close your finger over the tip and extract the straw. Now you have different layers of crushed ice in the straw. Similarly, scientists drill down into ice accumulated over centuries and extract an ice core. Ice has air bubbles trapped in it. Scientists measure carbon dioxide in this air.

ACKNOWLEDGEMENTS

Sohini Mitra, and all the people at Penguin India: Thank you for giving this book a chance! Shalini Agrawal, for the excellent edits!

My parents: Lifelong students themselves, they raised me to be curious, to question, to want to know more about everything. They pointed out to us science in everyday life. I owe to them my love for science (and the intense craving to write a book like this one).

Somewhere, somehow, this book must have been influenced by my grandfather J.R. Lakshmana Rao, a respected popular science writer in Kannada. It cannot be a coincidence that writing about science attracts me so much. Even if it wasn't directly his influence, it is largely due to him that my extended family is science-and-evidence-loving, and growing up in that atmosphere helped. Thanks especially to my aunt Anu Jagalur, adviser, editor and comforter. I'm also grateful to Anil Jagalur for running his expert eye over the manuscript.

Avani, whose sunshine lights up my world, listened patiently and gave me pertinent suggestions as I read out great tracts of the manuscript to her. As always, huge thanks to Sandesh for understanding my sudden silences and obsessive writing periods during which I was lost to the world around me.

REFERENCES

The Story of Science: Aristotle Leads the Way by Joy Hakim

The Story of Science: Newton at the Center by Joy Hakim

The Story of Science: Einstein Adds a New Dimension by Joy Hakim

The Story of Inventions by Anna Claybourne and Adam Larkum

Girls Think of Everything: Stories of Ingenious Inventions by Women by Catherine Thimmesh

Mistakes that Worked: 40 Familiar Inventions and How They Came to Be by Charlotte Foltz Jones and John O'Brien

Science: A History of Discovery in the Twentieth Century by Trevor I. Williams

The Short History of Nearly Everything by Bill Bryson